CHRIS LIPPINCOTT

SPIRITS BESIDE US

Gain Healing and Comfort from Loved Ones in the Afterlife

First published by Glossarium 2020

First edition

ISBN: 978-1-7347462-1-1

Editing by Candace Johnson
Cover art by Geoff Borin

This book was professionally typeset on Reedsy.
Find out more at reedsy.com

I dedicate this book to all my family members in spirit, especially my parents, who have inspired me and helped me come to understand the afterlife. Without spirit's inspiration, this book never could have been written. I further dedicate this book to my loving spirit guides who have helped me realize and unfold my spiritual nature and develop my abilities, and keep me on the endless path of growth and learning.

Namaste

"The spirit is beyond destruction. No one can bring an end to the spirit which is everlasting."

BHAGAVAD GITA

Contents

Foreword

I grew up in South Africa with a very logical mind. I could prove my point of view and back it up with loads of evidence. As a result, I spent the majority of my adult life as an attorney. However, my life took a surprising turn, and I found myself in the most illogical of pursuits; working with the spirit world. Now I seek evidence not in the courtroom but in my mediumship readings, and for the last twelve years I have been teaching classes in mediumship and psychic development.

I've seen Chris work in public demonstrations and in private readings, and he's quite good. He's given me readings where he's accurately brought through my family members and their messages. I've also seen Chris grow as a medium in my development circles, and its clear spirit is guiding him. When he initially told me he'd written a book about mediumship and asked me to read it, I thought it was just going to be yet another book on the topic. At first, I didn't think it was going to shed any light or do much for anyone.

However, I was stunned when I read Chris' book. Those who know me realize that's not something that happens easily. I couldn't put down the book because the moment I began reading it I was captivated by how he practically put me in his shoes during his readings and experiences. I felt and saw what he was experiencing, and it was almost palpable. This is no dry book on mediumship, this is a detailed journey into the spirit realm. Even with my many years as a medium and tutor, I felt I gained something reading this book.

What I found so interesting is how well Chris is able to weave together his over twenty years of personal research on the spirit world with his experiences as a medium. As a result, he is able to fluently articulate what spirit is, how the spirit world works, how we can communicate with spirit, and what our spirit loved ones are trying to let us know. Chris clearly describes that our family and friends in spirit are full of love and that the spirit realm is much closer than we realize.

Some of the most poignant moments in the book for me included Chris' spiritual journey as well as the incredibly moving readings that he provides. He takes the reader through his amazing evolution from agnostic materialist to spiritual medium, which I found so powerful. It's easy for someone to say they've always believed or they were brought up thinking spiritually. But when someone goes from skeptic to believer to practitioner, the potent transformation sends shivers down your spine. You begin to realize that there are greater forces at work guiding us in ways we never previously contemplated.

I loved the descriptions of his numerous readings with clients that tangibly demonstrate how our spirit loved ones heal us with their transformational love. Chris puts the reader in his mind and body, enabling us to viscerally feel, know and see everything that happens to him throughout the reading. We intimately know how spirit connects with him and what it's like for spirit to work through him. We get to see how the recipient of the reading is transformed, which pulls at every ounce of our emotions and opens our hearts. Consequently, we too are transformed by spirits' eternal love.

I'm very busy with my work as a medium and founder

of The MontClair Psychic School which is focused on the development of psychics, mediums and healers. I normally don't have time to read books. However, I found *Spirits Beside Us* so compelling, I had to read it, and I'm glad I did. Chris is not only a good medium, he's a great author and wordsmith. He is able to take a subject many find incomprehensible or unbelievable and turns it into an easy to understand piece of our everyday life, supported with a theme of love. I strongly encourage anyone remotely curious about the afterlife or what happens after our physical body dies to read this book. You will be happy you did.

Lee VanZyl - Director, Medium and Reiki Master
www.MontClairPsychicSchool.com

Acknowledgement

I'd like to acknowledge my great mentors and tutors who truly helped me develop my mediumship and pushed me to always step outside my comfort zone in an effort to forever grow and learn. You expanded my knowledge and understanding more than I ever dreamed possible. You never let me settle for anything less than the best and always encouraged me to be better than you were—the true mark of a great mentor. To you I express my heartfelt and most sincere thanks. I'd like to express my sincerest appreciation to my editor, Candace. You helped me pull this book together and made it flow well so that it was readable and enjoyable. I also want to express my deepest appreciation to my beloved wife, Carol. You had to endure my personal evolution and periods of uncertainty as I underwent my journey, yet you always stood by my side and supported my efforts. I never could have done any of this without you. I love you with all my heart, now and forever.

Tony Stockwell Tony is an international psychic medium, author, teacher and speaker with a career spanning thirty years. He is a certificate holder of the Spiritualist National Union award (CSNU) in teaching, demonstrating, and speaking. Tony is an approved tutor at England's renowned Arthur Findlay College-Stansted Hall, thought by many to be the home of British Spiritualism.

James Van Praagh James is a pioneer in the field of mediumship with thirty years of experience and is a highly respected spiritual teacher. A bestselling author, James is sought out by students around the world for his tutelage. He is a faculty fixture at the Omega Institute for Wellness in Rhinebeck, New York and offers courses through his online School of Mystical Arts.

Martin Twycross Martin is an internationally known teaching medium based in the United Kingdom. He has been teaching mediumship since 2006, holds the certificate of the Spiritualist National Union (CSNU) award in demonstrating and speaking, and is an approved tutor at England's Arthur Findlay College.

Rev. Janet Nohavec Rev. Janet is internationally known for her evidential mediumship. She is an approved overseas tutor for the prestigious Arthur Findlay College in Stansted, England. A former Roman Catholic nun, she has been featured extensively on television, radio and printed press. Her evidential form of mediumship has been researched by several university groups.

Lee VanZyl Lee is an international teaching medium with extensive training at the Arthur Findlay College, United Kingdom. Lee is a member of the International Spiritualist Federation. She has trained and taught classes at the Woodlands Foundation in Australia and New Zealand. Lee has been teaching mediumship and healing development since 2007 and is the founder of the MontClair Psychic School, which is focused on the development of psychics, mediums, and healers.

FREE
10 Ways Spirit Tries to Reach Us

As a way of saying thank you for your purchase, here is an article I wrote on ways that spirit tries to reach us. Click on the link below.

10 Ways Spirit Tries To Reach Us

Introduction

Jane walked with speed and determination into my dining room, as if this would bring her closer to the answers she sought. As we exchanged pleasantries and chatted about funny events of the day that spring of 2019, her words breathlessly spewed forth at a slightly elevated pitch, belying a heightened sense of eagerness and anticipation at what was to come. The twenty-four-year-old sat at the dining table where I conducted many of my mediumship readings and leaned forward as if those few inches might bring her closer to spirit. Her eyes stayed glued to mine, searching for someone else who might lie in wait behind my pupils. As I did before all my readings, I described the process for communicating with spirit, told Jane not to feed me any information, and limit her responses to yes, no, or maybe. We opened the session with a prayer.

I then cleared my mind and shifted my attention to the spirit world. On the dark, empty stage that filled my mind, a fuzzy image of a young man who looked like he was in his twenties or thirties slowly came into focus. A green Boston Celtics jersey cut off at the midsection fell loosely from his shoulders. Gray cotton shorts that came down to his knees didn't hide the slight paunch of his stomach. Red high-top sneakers covered his feet and announced his presence. The short hair on the top of his head stood up like recently cut blades of grass on a neatly manicured lawn. The sides were cut extremely short, almost bald, like you might see in a styled crew cut. Stubble darkened his round face. As he grew closer to me and unfolded his essence, he shared with me the understanding and familiarity so common between friends and acquaintances rather than the family bond of a brother. I described everything I saw and felt.

"Jane, do you recognize this man?"

"Yes, but his hair was less of a crew cut and more closely trimmed."

"Wow, is she getting picky," I thought to myself.

As I encouraged this young man to blend his spirit with mine and overshadow me, the pace of my heartbeat increased and pulsations of excited energy flowed through my arms and torso, causing bouncy mannerisms and changing vocal intonations. A subtle smirk crossed my lips, and I tilted my head slightly to the right as my eyes narrowed. After I urged him to let me know his personality, I virtually inhaled a heightened degree of self-confidence mixed with street smarts, together with a certain swagger you might find in a rough neighborhood. Jane said this characterization of her friend's personality and demeanor was quite accurate.

I asked him how he passed. Against a dark backdrop in my head, an empty orange pill bottle materialized, lying on its side with its opening pointing to the right. Its white cap lay off to the right. Where were the pills? Why would a pill bottle not have any pills in it … unless they'd all been taken already. To me, that's often a symbol of an overdose.

"I'm seeing an empty pill bottle, but there are no pills anywhere. I feel like they were all consumed at once. The image makes me think this young man died from an overdose. Does that make sense to you?"

"Yes. He committed suicide."

Small teardrops glistened in the light as they slowly formed in the corners of Jane's eyes. I silently asked this young man to let me know his age when he passed. To ascertain someone's age at passing, I normally move my hand along a timeline broken into decades until an overwhelming force in my mind compels me to stop. However, I didn't even have enough time to use my typical method. Instead, I suddenly wanted to begin talking about the number twenty-four, though I didn't know why initially.

"I just want to say the number twenty-four now, but I don't know what it means. I'm beginning to feel that it has to do with someone's age. Does the age twenty-four make sense to you in some way?" I blurted out.

"I'm twenty-four," Jane offered.

"No, it's for someone else, I think. It feels like someone's age, and it's just hitting me like a ton of bricks."

Jane suddenly gasped. "Oh my God! My friend who you were describing was twenty-four when he died!"

We both thought about that for a moment.

I then asked Jane's friend how I could best describe him in a way she would understand. In my mind, I saw her friend sitting on the floor of an empty basketball court that had a green emblem or logo on it, though I couldn't make out what it was. A huge, empty stadium or arena surrounded this basketball court. This didn't make any sense to me.

"I see your friend sitting on an empty basketball court that has a green logo on it, inside a big empty arena. Does this mean anything to you?"

Jane again drew in a short breath.

"Yes! This makes complete sense now. My friend was a die-hard Boston Celtics fan, so that's why he is wearing that jersey. The basketball court he's sitting on is in the stadium where the team plays. That's TD Garden in Boston! That logo you saw on the floor of the basketball court is the Celtics logo."

The young man got up and began moving in what at first looked like strange jerking motions. The closer I looked, the more I realized he was doing some kind of unique dance step or maybe some hip-hop dance. As he continued to overshadow me, I just wanted to start doing the same moves. I started laughing and swaying from side to side and dragging my index and middle fingers together across my eyes, one hand after the other, in opposite directions out to the sides. It looked like I was rhythmically sashaying to some imaginary dance beat. When Jane saw me doing this, she burst out laughing at how ridiculous I looked.

After she calmed down, Jane said, "That's one of my friend's favorite dance moves. He always did that at clubs when we went out dancing. It's called 'raving.' "

What did I know? At least Jane confirmed another piece of evidence from her friend in spirit.

The young man soon began giving Jane messages, which came in small bursts.

"You know I'm with you all the time."

"I'm always watching over you."

"I'm sorry I left the way I did. It was stupid, and I'm responsible for it, not you."

As she wiped a tear from her eye, Jane just nodded her head.

He pantomimed the idea, "Listen to your heart" as he pointed to his ear, then his heart, and then repeatedly back and forth.

"I totally understand that. My friend was trying to tell me to open up my heart again, since I completely shut down after he died.

We closed the session with a prayer.

"Chris, thank you so much. That was incredible hearing from him again."

"Thank your friend. He's the one who did all the hard work. It's pretty clear he's still a very close friend to you. He's watching you closely and not leaving your side."

Jane's wonderful reading yet again affirmed my faith in spirit's love for us and the fact that our loved ones in spirit are always with us and watching over us.

* * *

If you're reading this, you may have felt compelled to investigate spirit communication after the passing of a loved one, or maybe you're interested in it as a result of personal curiosity. Either way, I'm thrilled to share with you all the knowledge I've gained over the years about the spirit world and the ability to communicate with spirit. Together, we'll share a wonderful journey.

In this book I'll cover what spirit is, our relation to spirit, what spirit tells us about their world, the fundamentals of spirit communication, and what spirit is trying to tell us. I'll also relay the stories of some remarkable readings and how sitters' lives have changed when they reconnect with their loved ones in spirit. You'll also learn the journey of how I became a medium, how the experience has shaped me, and much more.

As you read this book, you may begin to feel closer to spirit, come to understand that spirit is actually much closer than you previously imagined, and start gaining a different perspective on this life and the next. You may begin to feel more spiritual and closer to Divine Source Energy that loves us and guides us all. Throughout this book I try to use terms like Divine Source Energy, Source, the Divine, or any combination of those in addition to "God" to avoid sounding overly religious, for that occasionally turns off some people.

Religion versus Spirituality

Please recognize that spirituality references our personal and internal relation with a higher power, whereas religion is more outside of our self, less personal, and institutional. Religion includes a set of belief systems, creeds, and dogma, unlike spirituality, which is one's own beliefs and quite personal. Please don't think I'm trying to put down any religions or people who feel religious—on the contrary. I think religion can be very supportive. However, I do feel it's important to highlight the difference between spirituality and religion as we begin our quest for spirit.

Martin Twycross, CSNU, has described spiritual development as "A process by which a person achieves greater awareness of their true spiritual nature and a greater connection to all things, including the Divine."[1] Before I began my journey to become a medium, I certainly wasn't spiritual or religious, but now I've learned so much I can't help but be significantly more spiritual. I think you may grow in a similar way. You may, in fact, begin to learn how to communicate with spirit by yourself!

Now what do you think of when you hear the phrase *psychic medium*? Do you envision a person with a crystal ball on their table or a purple neon sign hanging in their shop window that reads "Psychic," or a sandwich board on the street advertising a five-dollar reading? Perhaps you might be skeptical and question that person's validity, honesty, and ability to communicate with spirit. You may even question their sanity.

The Difference Between Psychics and Mediums

People often confuse the differences between psychics and mediums, and they lump them all together. Psychics receive most of their information from people on earth (spirit incarnate) and their aura, whereas mediums receive information from people in the spirit world (spirit discarnate). Both use their psychic senses to receive the information, but a medium needs to link with spirit to get information, while a psychic links with people still here on earth. Importantly, a medium uses spiritual power to create that link, unlike a psychic, who does not. Power is essentially the fuel to create a good connection with spirit. In short, a medium equals a psychic plus power to receive a connection with spirit. As the saying goes, all mediums are psychic, but not all psychics are mediums.

Types of Mediums

Mediums practice two fundamental types of mediumship: mental mediumship and physical mediumship. Mental mediumship is the most common form of mediumship and is, in most cases, subjective. This includes evidential mediumship (the majority of the reading is evidence, the balance is messages), trance mediumship (where the medium goes into a trance, allowing the spirit communicator to speak), spirit art (where the medium allows the spirit to draw or paint, even if the medium himself has no talent) and automatic writing (where spirit overshadows the author and writes its desired text, typically without the human instrument knowing what is being written).

Physical mediumship, quite rare in modern times, is objective. This includes materialization/dematerialization, percussion/raps, apports (where spirit brings objects from the other side to the physical plane), transfiguration (where the spirit marks its face over the face of the medium), levitation, telekinesis (such as table tipping) and electronic voice phenomena (EVP). Physical mediumship was quite popular in the later part of the nineteenth century and early part of the twentieth century. However, this lost popularity due to cases of fraudulent activities and the increasing pace of life in modern times that left physical mediums less able to focus on their craft.

Most mental mediums are quite honest, deeply caring, and truly capable. They have carefully developed their ability to communicate with spirit over a number of years and are quite sane, despite the protestations of some skeptics. Most are quite spiritual and seek ways they can serve others, for mediumship at its core is a calling to help others, both in spirit and in the flesh. Mediums come from all walks of life. They have different backgrounds, diverse personalities, and are of different religions. In fact, we all have psychic abilities. But like many things, some people have developed their capabilities while others have let them lie dormant. The vast majority of mediums are regular people who have simply developed their psychic senses and unfolded their spiritual nature so they are able to communicate with spirit.

For example, I'm the last thing you'd imagine if you thought of the word *medium*. I look more like the average middle-aged man who might be coming home from a day at the office. I've got a beautiful wife and a fantastic teenage son; I live in a busy New Jersey suburb close to New York City, and I live life like everyone else. I certainly don't seem to fit many people's preconceived notion of a medium—if such a thing even exists anymore. Even some of my friends don't know I communicate with those who are no longer in the physical realm … or are quite surprised when I tell them. "You're the *last* person I would've guessed would be a medium!" they exclaim.

How I Came to Mediumship

I never went looking for spirit; they found me. I was led by the nose to mediumship by spirit that had a very different agenda than I did. Looking back on my childhood, it occurs to me now that I was quite aware of spirit; I just never fully realized what spirit was trying to do. Back then I perceived spirit more like a Hollywood ghost story or an invasion of monsters. As a child, I was scared to death when spirit tried to contact me. Consequently, I suppressed my abilities for nearly three decades.

Eventually spirit realized I was ready to become reacquainted with it and began slowly placing enticing nuggets of information before me, kind of like breadcrumbs, which I eagerly followed. It started with interesting book titles that caught my attention over the course of twenty years of reading. Then it slowly evolved into a growing fascination with metaphysics, spirituality, and the afterlife. Soon, key events in my life changed me, and I experienced a spiritual reawakening that brought spirit fully into my life for good.

No matter how much I avoided it or had trouble believing it, the spirit world chose me as one of their ambassadors because it saw something in me that was helpful in their quest to raise human consciousness. Never in a million years would I ever have seen myself as a medium. Yet here I am, happily communicating with people in the spirit world who are just like they were when they were with us on earth. Now, it takes just a bit more effort to hear and communicate with them.

I absolutely love communicating with spirit. Their messages are based on love, caring, concern for others, regret for what they might have done while on earth or how they might have hurt others, and how they might have lived a better life. They frequently express their love to their family and friends and encourage them to live their life to the fullest. What's notable about spirit is their lack of ego, for they leave behind their ego and retain only their loving consciousness.

Spirit truly does see life from "the other side" and gives us great perspective on how we can live better lives ourselves. We really can learn a thing or two from those that have gone before us and are now trying to teach us lessons. In fact, there's a Divine reason you picked up this book, and spirit may be trying to reach you with a message already. Always remember, there's never any such thing as a coincidence. So ready or not, let's get started!

—*Chris Lippincott*

I

Is Spirit Real?

1

My Early Journey

"The journey of a thousand miles begins with one step."
—Lao Tzu

On a late summer evening in rural Connecticut when I was seven, I lay in my bed tossing and turning, unable to fall asleep. The late night created a darkness that swallowed everything whole, preventing me from seeing my hand in front of my face. I searched in vain for a sound, but the empty countryside offered nothing but silence. Except for the rustling of my sheets I heard when I moved, I might as well have been in a deprivation chamber. As an only child, I didn't have to worry about annoying siblings playing jokes on me. However, that night I sure could have used someone there to chat with to allay my fears. My parents were at the other end of our long house, so they couldn't help me. Once they tucked me in and closed my bedroom door, they might as well as have been on another continent.

But I was seven. I was a big boy. I didn't have to worry; nothing could hurt me.

That's when I heard it.

A soft whisper in the middle of my room. I froze. Was someone else there? I didn't remember hearing or seeing the door open. The voice sounded like a man, or maybe a cunning monster, but how'd he get in? Maybe if I didn't move, he wouldn't see me.

Then I heard it again, closer this time. I thought this thing was approaching my bed, so I had to do something fast. I slid farther down my bed, threw the covers over my head, and begged him to just go away, while my entire body shook like a leaf. The voice wasn't menacing, but just the fact that it appeared out of thin air in the middle of the night made me think it had to be dangerous. I couldn't tell what the man was saying, but he must have been speaking to me since I was the only person in the room.

The voice faded away after a few minutes of my pleading with it to leave. By that point my heart was up in my throat, and I could barely think straight. I contemplated making a mad dash for it out of my room and into the safety of my parents' arms, but I wasn't sure if the man was still there. Worse yet, perhaps monsters might be lurking about ready to grab me. Didn't all monsters come from underneath the bed or out from the closet at night?

I heard the voice a few more times that summer, but it never really stuck around more than a minute. Then my nights went back to normal, and I felt like I could finally get a good night's rest. Of course I began to keep one eye open … or at least pay attention to what was out beyond my bed. That seemed to work, for once I did, I didn't hear the voice again for the rest of the summer. At last I was safe and sound, and no more monsters or scary things could attack me.

Then the contact got personal.

One night during the fall I was lying on my stomach and finally drifting off to sleep when the distinct pressure on the middle of my back of a hand with its five fingers and palm alerted me to certain danger. I panicked, thinking that the monsters in my room were coming to take me back to their lair at last. Every fiber of my being lay frozen in fear. I couldn't move a muscle. The hand didn't move; it just calmly rested on my back. Still, I wasn't having any of it, and I begged it to leave. After a few moments, the hand disappeared as unexpectedly as it had arrived. Maybe it heard my pleas. This happened multiple times over the course of the fall.

Each time I begged whatever force was behind the hand to remove it from my back. I was practically in tears I was so afraid. Finally after my desperate and continued appeals to the hand never to return, it listened to me. I never felt it again. Nor did I ever hear the voice again. At last my prayers had been answered. I was safe.

Like the three ghosts in *A Christmas Carol,* spirit sent a third ambassador to my house. The final entity to greet me surrounded my body with an energetic presence. This time, however, the new being followed me wherever I went after the sun went down. It wasn't limited just to my bed anymore. In my young mind, if it was happening after dark, then it had to be bad.

I remember the first appearance occurred on a late fall evening as I walked through our living room, which had been constructed from a long, converted two-story barn. I was about midway through the massive room when a ball of energy completely wrapped around me and created a massive tingling sensation up and down my torso. Uncertain about what this energy field was, I tried to run away in panic as I became convinced that it must be some dangerous, invisible creature trying to hurt me. Of course the giant portrait in front of me, of a man from the nineteenth century with glaring eyes that followed my every move, only contributed to my hysteria. As I desperately jumped into my parents' arms in another room, the energy ball evaporated.

The second visitation occurred at bedtime a few days later. Again I lay on my stomach, and I sensed the energy cover my back, arms, and legs like an invisible cloud of electricity hovering over my body. Everything started to tingle like warm goosebumps or millions of tiny fingers lightly tapping all over me. I sensed the electric energy the most in my upper arms, though it also wrapped around my chest and back like a warm blanket of effervescent bubbles. I was certain this energy field, like the voice and the hand, somehow was connected to *somebody,* though I didn't know how.

After a few more encounters with that invisible electric cloud and my constant begging for it to stop, I didn't feel it anymore. Maybe it moved on to where it might be more respected or desired. Once I realized these entities had left and would never return, though, I walked aimlessly about my house with a dejected gaze on the floor and my shoulders hunched over. I wasn't sure if I felt upset because I'd rejected some personal connection to something larger than me or if it was the reaction of a lonely only child looking for a playmate. My gut suggested it was larger than me.

I had no way of knowing these experiences were really a door that opened into another world, one that I had slammed shut as a result of my childhood fears.

* * *

Many people have asked me how or when I knew I was a medium. Some assume I just "knew," or I'd always been able to communicate with spirit people since childhood. While that may be true for some mediums, many actually don't fully develop their sensitivity until later in life. This was essentially what happened to me; I didn't develop this talent until I was an adult.

Like most kids, I didn't give spirit much thought when I was young (aside from those few unusual experiences). I always had my fantasy playmates and invisible friends during the daytime, and I thought that's what everyone had to just pass the time. I thought we all made up playmates to keep ourselves occupied or from feeling lonely. I desperately needed someone to play with, so that's what I did, to the point of having animated conversations with invisible friends and elements of nature like trees, animals, and plants.

I spoke with anything that was near me and seemed to be alive, so long as the sun was up. That way I knew it wasn't a dangerous monster. Little did I know that I was actually in contact with spirit through my fantasy playmates and the energy in the animals and trees. To me they were very alive, but I didn't think they were anything different than just my "friends." Of course, when my playmates could carry on full conversations with me and respond, that should have told me something. However, I thought I just had a terrific imagination, which in hindsight probably allowed me to be open to spirit.

I was also quite hyperactive. While all children are high energy at that age, I seemed to carry an energy level above the norm. I couldn't sit still for a moment. It was a challenge for me to focus, though I could when I needed to. I was always bouncing from place to place and project to project. I was like a device using a car battery that only accepted single A batteries. Too much energy flooded the motor. It just felt like I was constantly on overdrive. Looking back on things now, it makes complete sense that I could detect higher vibrational beings, as my vibrational movements were higher than normal due to my hyperactivity.

As I grew older and more skeptical of everything around me, I let go of what I considered "childish" fantasies and make-believe playmates, just as most children do. I lost touch with the spirit world as my analytical and materialistic mind formed and began to squeeze out my creative and spiritual mind. Logic and rules of the physical world took over. My parents weren't particularly religious or spiritual, so I grew up focused more on the material world. I just continued on my way as a normal, self-centered, and materialistic only child. Yet I never could completely forget those childhood instances of talking to invisible playmates, communicating with the natural world, and experiencing those encounters at night.

The nighttime energies and sensations of a presence continued to occur even when I became a young adult, though not to quite the same degree. As a result, I thought I must have some subconscious fear of the dark. Still, I wasn't aware of the concept that spirits might be trying to contact me or trying to awaken me to any abilities I might naturally possess. I'd heard that mediums existed, but I always thought they must be superhuman with rare, magical gifts. I didn't really know much, if anything, about them. As a result, I thought I was just an adult man who was excessively afraid of the dark.

However, as the years progressed I was becoming inexplicably curious about the afterlife, spirits, near-death-experien ces (NDEs), and people with mediumistic abilities. Over the course of the last twenty-five years, I've acquired a voracious appetite for all things spirit-related. It started with NDEs and reincarnation. They were more tangible than spirit, and people were coming back to talk about their experiences. As a result, I could believe much of what these people were saying about their NDEs.

It wasn't all that farfetched in my mind, especially if universities were lending credibility to the authors' experiences, including the Rhine Research Center at Duke University and the University of Virginia's Division of Perceptual Studies. So I kept reading everything I could get my hands on. This included descriptions of NDEs, books about reincarnation, academic studies, and scientific research, all of which appeared to support the concept that human consciousness survives death. However, my interests and my reading list kept evolving over time.

One morning when I was in my late forties, I rode the bus to New York City. Though still interested in NDEs, I wondered what the spirit world was really like as I sat bored in my seat. The bus slowed down as it entered a curved exit ramp between Routes 3 and 495 near the Lincoln Tunnel and then waited in a long line behind other buses. I happened to peer out my window to the right, and there in front of me stood a huge billboard advertising a new book. It captured my attention because it displayed a large scene of the dark night sky illuminated by millions of bright stars shining their light at the viewer. I couldn't take my eyes off of it. All it said was *The Light Between Us: Stories From Heaven. Lessons for the Living* by Laura Lynne Jackson.

Something inside me suddenly clicked. I stared at the billboard, captivated by what I saw. A subtle voice inside my head urged me to read this book, and hinted that this billboard had been placed here so that I would see it. This occurred around the same time my fascination with spirit was growing exponentially, so I recognized the uncanny synchronicity. I knew this was more than sheer coincidence. I don't have a great memory, but I memorized that book title and ordered it as soon as I got home. At that point, it seems, the flood gates essentially burst open.

Before I realized it, I was reading everything I could get my hands on about spirit and the afterlife. I scoured the internet and explored library shelves in search of any relevant book I could find. I read automatic writings by spirit authors and trance recordings on how spirit transitioned from the physical to the nonphysical, what their world was like, how they lived, how they contacted us, and detailed stories about mediums and their abilities. I read numerous studies and scientific theorems from quantum physicists, researchers, psychiatrists, and scientists that not only explained the science behind spirit, but also validated the continuation of consciousness beyond physical death. Piles of information poured over me as if shot from a fire hose, shouting to be heard as evidence for life after life.

The timing of everything happening in perfect order still astonishes me. While I was reading and learning more about spirit, I unexpectedly came across a website that rationally presented the idea of meditation as a way to calm myself and progress along my spiritual path. Had I seen this website before reading about spirit, I would have ignored it due to my materialist bent. Now, after everything I'd read, it piqued my curiosity.

Given my analytical mind, I had to learn everything about

meditation—how it worked and its importance on health and spiritual growth. I started practicing with different guided meditations and soundtracks that website offered in an effort to help relieve my stress from work and family life. I remember thinking that meditation was very peaceful and relaxing, but I never expected anything profound to happen, as I still wasn't fully on board with anything spiritual.

However, things started to change when I began to meditate more consistently and developed a daily meditation practice. I started to realize there were bigger forces in the universe that I hadn't accepted previously. As a materialist with no real religious or spiritual upbringing, I had trouble fully believing in God or Jesus or angels, since I needed proof they existed. How could anyone believe in these entities based on faith alone, I asked myself, since people can't see them? I thought they were people's attempts to find explanations for inexplicable occurrences. To me, this was akin to prehistoric man attributing rain to one god and drought to another god. Modern man had just consolidated all the many different gods into one for convenience, hadn't he? Worse yet, my cynicism back then faulted the church. I thought it was power hungry, taking advantage of people's fears.

As I started meditating daily, however, my viewpoint began to evolve, and my mind slowly opened to other possibilities. I began to find certain guided meditations that presented concepts of a warm, loving and benevolent light that would gently surround me, protect me, and fill me with love. It had no name, no agenda, no dogma, and no creed or set of belief systems to follow. It was just there, like a patient, kindly, loving parent. *What was not to like?* To me, this amiable light seemed like a pretty good thing, and I could accept it.

I didn't really know what it was, but it certainly didn't require me to believe in anything or force-feed me a strict religious system. This light emanated from somewhere beyond the universe and required me to use a little bit of my imagination, much the way I did when I was a child. I began to like this loving light and started to seek it more often, even though I still didn't realize what it was. This warm light had a friendly, welcoming personality that I could connect with whenever I needed someone, much the way I behaved in my childhood. While I loved my wife and son, they naturally and understandably had their own agendas.

My Spirit Guides

I'd heard of spirit guides in my twenties, but paid no attention since I was still a staunch materialist at the time and thought they were religious beings similar to guardian angels. However, two decades later I was opening to new ideas because of everything I'd read and my meditation practice. I began to search for my spirit guides as I grew more philosophical, and I thought they might help me with my spiritual growth. Fortunately, I had started to keep a journal of my experiences (in case anything remarkable might happen), though I never seriously considered there would be any notable entries.

I didn't have a clue how I might get in contact with my guides. I began by looking online for ways to connect, but nothing I read or heard resonated with me. Worse, many of the people I saw giving instructions on how to reach one's spirit guides just seemed straight out of central casting for a bad fortune teller, and I couldn't take them or their suggestions seriously.

One woman in a video literally had a turban on her head, wore gaudy colorful clothes like a gypsy, had a crystal ball on a circular table, which was covered by a blue table cloth that had stars all over it. As she fondly rubbed her crystal ball, she began moaning and chanting while her voice got low and mysterious. Then she gasped with wide eyes and said she'd connected with her spirit guides. I began laughing so hard that I had to wipe tears off my face as I struggled to catch my breath. I knew this was definitely *not* how to connect.

So I tried meditating by just sitting with my eyes closed and inviting the warm and loving light that some of the guided meditations had introduced me to and mentally sending thoughts out to my guides. It started more like an experiment. I had zero expectations and thought, "There's no way this can possibly work." Needless to say, I set a very low bar for success.

Perhaps that was a good thing because I didn't make any contact for a very long time, so I wasn't disappointed. Also, I thought that if I did hear anything, it would probably be my own mind speaking back to me and just tricking me. Yet one day in late July of 2015, after sitting like I normally did and trying to reach my guides for what seemed like an eternity, I got the strange energetic and tingling feeling that I hadn't felt since I was a child.

At first I thought I was just cold and getting goosebumps, and maybe even imagining it. However, I realized I wasn't cold, and these weren't goosebumps. The sensation enveloped me like a very gentle, warm, almost champagne-like tingling in a thin band at the very top and side of my arms. I imagined light, bubbly hands were softly placed on either side of my shoulders.

At this point, my heart started racing. I thought I felt some kind of energy or a presence in front of me, so I guardedly peeked out of one eye to see what was there. I only saw an empty room, so I closed my eye and doubled my attention on what I was feeling.

I silently asked, "Is anybody there?"

No response.

"Are you my spirit guide?"

Nothing.

Undeterred, I continued to sit and listen for anything that might suggest something or *somebody* was there.

I began to think back to my childhood experiences when mysterious, disembodied hands would touch my back at night and I felt energetic presences draw near me. The feelings around me now were exactly same. All my childhood memories came flooding back to me about my conversations with my invisible friends and connections with the energy in nature. I had a Eureka moment when it occurred to me that I was now experiencing the very same thing. I became more confident that something magnificent was happening, and I felt compelled to learn what it was.

Finally, I asked in my mind, "If you're my spirit guide, can you give me a name?"

To my complete and utter shock, I suddenly felt or heard internally, "Judy."

I was simultaneously ecstatic and let down. I was ecstatic because at last I'd received a response confirming I was connecting to my spirit guide, but let down because the name seemed so ordinary. I thought a spirit guide was supposed to have some fancy, ancient and wise-sounding name, like Great Eagle or Amenmeses or Rutasashaka. But *Judy*?

That didn't sound too all-knowing to me. It sounded pretty

common. How could a guide with a name like "Judy" possibly help anyone? Worse yet, I immediately began to doubt the experience and thought it must be my imagination or just the internal voice I heard every day when I talked to myself. I thought I also heard the name "Frank" as a secondary guide, but I was so disheartened with another common name that I just chalked that up to my imagination. Strangely, I saw in my mind an image of an eagle's eye in the forefront, with a lion image behind that and a crocodile in the background. I had no concept what these images meant initially, so I thought it was more imagination run amok. However, I'd uncover their significance later.

For a few weeks, I gave up trying to communicate with my guides and went back to my skeptic frame of mind again. But the initial experience and its similarity to my childhood memories was too much for me to ignore. Those memories egged me on. One month after my initial contact, I went back to sitting for my guides. I thought perhaps I must have annoyed the guides with my skepticism because, just like before, it appeared to take forever to make any connection. Then one day, once again, I got that fizzy, energetic tingling around my shoulders and upper arms, and I jumped out of my skin with excitement.

"Are you my spirit guide? If you are, can you identify yourself?"

I lost some of my elation as I still wasn't getting any response. However, the energetic charge was still there, so I kept on trying.

I asked again. "Can you please give me your name?"

Inside my head I heard, "Judy."

I realized that again I'd made contact. Furthermore, it

dawned on me that I didn't know any Judy in my life, hadn't heard the name in years, and thought this name couldn't have come from my imagination. A huge grin crossed my face just for connecting with spirit.

For weeks I kept sitting for my guides. Initially, I never received much information or interaction from them. In my research, I'd read we can have up to as many as seven primary guides who work with us, so I began to ask if there were other guides present. I didn't hear about other guides or who was a lead guide or a secondary guide. I felt let down, like my guides weren't really there for me. I did hear the name "Frank" again, and I realized this wasn't my imagination anymore. I learned he was my secondary guide alerting me to his presence. I still keep his name in my group to this day.

Late that summer, after sitting for my guides without any results, everything changed. While in a deep meditation using a new soundtrack, I started feeling the tingling sensations around my upper arms that signaled Judy stood nearby. I soon sensed more energy focused on my head, and I thought someone had just plugged into my mind like an old switchboard operator from the 1930s. I heard Judy's voice.

"Follow your passion and your calling to love, to help, to heal, to care, and to teach. Follow your heart and your feelings, for they will illuminate your path."

This shocked me because I'd never really thought about those concepts. I was still at heart a stubborn materialist, though I was learning.

"Always follow love," she continued, "for love will show you the way. It is your mission to learn from the painful experiences in your life. Continue meditating, for it will prove to be a very powerful aid. Meditating will help you grow your spirit and allow you to see higher powers more clearly." Then Judy's voice trailed off, and her energetic vibration dissipated.

I sat in my armchair, stunned, my mind silent. I slowly brought myself back to a fully conscious state of awareness and tried to process everything I'd experienced. I quickly began thinking about the ramifications of everything I'd just heard.

"Isn't this the kind of stuff either great prophets or crazy people hear?" I asked myself. "I'm definitely no prophet, so ... oh my God." I panicked. "How can I hear such profound words from spirit if I'm just some normal person with no great abilities? Am I becoming unhinged?"

It didn't really make sense to me, but I kept meditating, just in case something good might come out of all this.

Later that fall, I again sat in meditation, but this time I envisioned myself enveloped in a golden ball of light emanating from my heart. It was quite warm and full of unconditional love. After a moment, I allowed myself to travel up a beam of white light from the crown of my head into the starry night sky. Unexpectedly, my perception and reality changed so that I was no longer in control of my imagination. I experienced a beautiful journey in which I traveled up within the beam of white light and arrived in a world covered in white light. However, there was no direct light source and there were no shadows, as everything radiated white light independently.

I wore a simple, lightweight white robe with a white rope loosely tied at the front, and sandals on my feet. As I looked around, everyone had varying styles and colors of robes, most of them illuminating some type of light. I worried others would think I was an imposter and didn't belong there. However, my entire body tingled with the effervescent, champagne-like energy that I'd come to associate with spirit, so I knew I wasn't entirely out of place.

I looked up a hill off to my left, and standing on top stood an enormous structure that reached far up into the sky. I stared at it in awe, overwhelmed with its beauty. Gigantic pointy spires rose up along the exterior walls of the building every twenty feet, each made out of massive, lengthy pieces of emerald that brilliantly sparkled in the light. It reminded me of the Emerald City in *The Wizard of Oz*.

No sooner was I staring at the structure in amazement than I found myself inside. I stood in what must have been the center hall, one that reminded me of a center hall in some huge old college library. It smelled of leather and old wood, and the feeling of overwhelming knowledge and intelligence pervaded every nook and cranny. I stood gawking at the building's interior.

Looking up, I saw countless book shelves in every direction rising hundreds of stories high, filled with every imaginable type of book and document, with doors at every level leading to rooms I couldn't see. Above the floor in the center hallway stood a spire open to the sky, from which brilliant white light streamed down onto the white marble floor. Embedded in the floor were four very narrow, black marble isosceles triangles, one pointing in each direction.

I brought my attention back down to the first floor and saw in front of me across the main entrance hall a large oak door with a shiny brass loop for a handle. On the door hung a sign that read Meeting In Progress. For some reason, I just walked over to the door and opened it, feeling like this meeting was for me, though I had absolutely no clue why.

I entered a large oval room, two stories tall. Multicolored

light streamed in through the floor-to-ceiling stained glass windows. Before me stood a huge oval table made of white marble, surrounded by eight large, ornately carved wooden chairs. Seven of the chairs were already filled with wise-looking men and women of different ages, whom I assumed had to be my spirit guides. They wore elaborate and brilliantly colored robes, many with gold and purple threads running throughout, some with tall, stiff collars, others with wide shoulders. They stood up and walked over to me and embraced me, emitting unconditional love and acceptance; it felt like a homecoming celebration.

I went around the room asking each guide what their names were, what they specialized in, and how I might recognize them. One guide who remained in the back left caught my attention. She looked like she was in her twenties, and had a pasty white face and a small head. She wore a long, flowing white dress with what looked like a very tall collar. The dress gleamed and appeared to emit some type of energy. Somehow, I thought I knew this woman, but I didn't know why or from where.

Only one guide, someone I didn't recognize, responded to my questions. "I'm here to guide you in learning your spiritual lessons," he said. "It's my task to help you stay on your spiritual path. This may take hard work and much practice on your part. However, there are many others who walk alongside you who will help you on your journey."

I didn't fully appreciate the meaning behind these messages until later.

2

My Awakening

"The awakening is finally realizing that you are a part of God, like a single cell that finally sees it is a part of you."
—L.J Vanier

Almost one year to the day after starting conversations with my spirit guides, a spiritual lightning bolt struck me from out of the ether. During a morning meditation one sunny weekend in July of 2016 in my man cave (we guys always have to have one somewhere), I'd progressed so well into my meditation that I reached an almost trance-like state. At that point I wasn't in a state of conscious analysis; it was more like a light sleepy awareness and acceptance. My mind and body were quite calm and relaxed, and I existed in a light, floating buoyancy.

The next thing I knew, I thought I'd been transported to some ethereal existence like heaven or the afterlife. In this altered state, I stood looking at four spirit people who were mostly in silhouette, backlit by a grayish light, yet somehow they seemed very tangible. The two beings facing me on the right side were taller than the two on the left, and they seemed to be substantially more energetic as well, almost as it they were higher beings somehow. I thought I knew them all, and I knew they were important, but I just couldn't place them.

At one point, the tallest spirit on the right shot a palpable beam of energy through my chest and out my back, though there was no sensation of discomfort. The sizzling, high energy of the beam dumbfounded me; if I was having a dream, I wondered, how could I feel something physically? I realized I wasn't dreaming. Everything around me suddenly emanated intense, pure, unconditional love. It existed everywhere around me, and my entire being pulsated with this high vibration of love energy. *I had become love and was one with this universe.* I realized the illusion of duality and separation, and I began to appreciate the reality of unity, that we are all connected as one energy. The love I felt surpassed anything I'd previously known or experienced. It was a sensation so overpowering and all-encompassing that the human word *love* doesn't even begin to describe it.

The simple word *love* just seemed like the tip of the iceberg compared to the full meaning of the love I was experiencing. The universe loved and accepted me just for existing, like a parent loves a young child. There was no right or wrong, no judgment, and nothing less than perfection. Somehow, these beings believed I was perfect. The spirit beings let me know that Source energy and the multiverse are one endless tapestry of pure love of which I was a fundamental part. They also pointedly told me that I was on my path of spiritual learning, and that's why I came to be incarnate in the physical. I came into this body from a spiritual realm to learn specific lessons that only this life could provide. I didn't fully understand what they were talking about until years later.

Once my communication with these beings concluded and I came back to my earthly reality, I sat in my chair for a good fifteen minutes trying to understand what I'd just experienced. I stood up, walked over to my desk, and desperately scribbled down everything I could remember from the meditation. I couldn't find words to accurately describe my feelings or the messages spirit had relayed to me, and I struggled to comprehend their meaning.

In subsequent days, unusual things began to happen to me. I perceived tingling sensations all over my body more frequently. I sensed energy around me and knew someone was there, but I just couldn't physically see them. I envisioned very clear images of both people and objects in my mind's eye. This was similar to imagining detailed pictures of objects or people against a large blank screen or dark room in my mind, yet somehow I knew what I saw wasn't just my imagination. I encountered unusual periods of calmness and peace more often in my everyday life, which was notable since I was still stressed out from my career and family life at the time. Additionally, my deceased relatives began to visit me in extremely vivid dreams, the details of which I still remember years later.

One night late that summer, for example, I dreamed I sat on my bed back in my childhood bedroom in Connecticut, though in my dream I was in my late forties. The sun stood high in the sky in the middle of the day. I could hear my wife talking to somebody in the kitchen next to my room, which I thought strange since she'd never seen my childhood home. I had to find out what was going on, so I got up and walked down the short hallway toward the kitchen. At the end of the hall I turned right to walk into the kitchen and see who was with my wife. The kitchen still contained a combination of early 1970s yellow walls and orange Formica countertops exactly as I remembered it from childhood. My wife sat at the right side of our old wooden kitchen table that rested against the center of the back wall. I turned my gaze slightly to my left and froze.

At the left side of the table sat my father, who had died thirty years earlier, in his light-blue cotton pajamas and lightweight dark-blue cotton bathrobe with his monogram on the left breast pocket. I drew in my breath so strongly from shock that my lower lip flapped against my upper teeth like a flag in the wind. Strangely, I even felt the physical sensation of my lips against my teeth as if I were awake.

I turned back to my wife in horror mixed with confusion, my eyes pleading with her as if to ask, "Is he really there?" She just nodded her head.

I looked back at my father and noticed he appeared so much healthier and younger than I remembered him. His skin was lightly tanned, his white hair neatly combed and closely trimmed, his physique lean and trim. Gone were the bleeding sores on his legs, the bloated stomach, the wrinkles and stubble on his face. He had died when he was sixty, yet here he sat before me in his forties. My father stood up and looked at me with a gentle smile on his face. Without moving his lips, he spoke to me.

"I'm so sorry I was such a poor father. I loved you so much, but I didn't know how to tell you."

I ran into his arms and silently yelled as forcefully as my mind would allow, "Daddy, I love you so much! You were the best father I ever could have hoped for. You were so talented, amazing, funny, and caring. I never would have wished for anything else. I'm sorry I ever made fun of you. You were right, I was an ungrateful teenager."

I squeezed him tightly and never wanted to leave his warm, protective embrace. I stood there in my father's arms sobbing uncontrollably with tears pouring down my face. I cried from elation just to be with my father again, and from agony because I knew he wasn't with me anymore.

I immediately awoke with tears on my face and realized I'd been crying. This experience was so vivid, explicit, and raw that it felt completely real, and I couldn't dismiss it as a regular dream. I woke up my wife to tell her everything I'd seen.

"Honey, did you also just have a dream where you sat at an old wooden kitchen table speaking with my father?"

Rubbing her eyes, she grumbled, "No, I didn't. But it sounds like your dream was more than your unconscious mind dealing with confusing thoughts. Maybe something important did happen to you, but I can't explain what."

One month later, another short but powerful dream visitation shook my belief system. I dreamed I stood on an ornate, graceful spiraling stairway, reminiscent of Versailles. Strangely the stairway, surrounded by empty black space, seemed to be floating. I began to climb it slowly, and about halfway up I saw an intricately carved rectangular mirror covered with gilding or gold paint, which stood vertically on the landing point where the staircase turned to go in the opposite direction. Stopping there to admire this masterpiece of centuries-old craftsmanship, I peered into the glass and gasped. In the reflection stood my deceased paternal grandmother at the top of the staircase.

I whipped around to get a better view of her. Looking regal in a fancy cocktail dress, she stood there staring down at me, her right arm at her side and her left hand gracefully holding the metal banister. She didn't look anything like the soft-spoken, eighty-eight -year old woman with curly white hair and small stature I recalled from my childhood. In fact, I couldn't visually recognize her, yet somehow I knew "Granny" was standing before me, alive and well.

She presented herself as a middle-aged woman with highly styled brown hair, narrow eyes that seemed to bore through me, a very strong personality, and an iron will. She also gave me the feeling that she had experienced tremendous heartache and emotional upheaval and still carried a torch for a long-lost love. However, I sensed she also cared deeply about her family members, including me.

"I love you," I heard her say without moving her lips.

"Granny, I love you too. I miss you terribly."

"Don't worry. I'm always with you."

Then I woke up, not quite sure what I'd just experienced, but my heart was beating a mile a minute, and my breath was fast and shallow. But again, this felt tangible, vivid, and raw, unlike nearly all of my prior dreams.

Not to be outdone, my father again let me know he was still around. Perhaps a few months after my grandmother visited me, my father appeared in another dream. This time I was in my late teens, and I was in my bedroom in our New York City apartment a few years after we'd moved there from Connecticut. It was evening, and I sat upright in my bed reading a book. The configuration of my bedroom was a bit odd.

My bed was on the left half of the rectangular room near the windows, with the headboard against one wall and the footboard facing the opposite wall. The room had two doors—one on the wall near the foot of my bed, the other on the opposite wall against which my headboard rested, but off to the right side of my room.

In my dream I was calmly reading a book in bed, but something caught my eye so I turned my head to my right. Just then my father passed straight through the door on my right. He was in perfect health and appeared to be in his forties, and he was as solid as everything in my room. This time, however, he carried four suitcases, one in each hand and one under each arm. He turned toward me and smiled. I smiled back. He continued moving diagonally across my room to the other door, the one near the foot of my bed. As he approached the door, he turned to smile at me again, turned back, and then disappeared through the door. I sat there, stunned. Then I woke up.

I guess my mother, who had passed over fifteen years before my awakening, felt that she too needed to say hello, because she visited me twice several months after my father appeared. One night I lay in bed on my right side trying to go to sleep. After closing my eyes, I began to enter the hypnagogic state of consciousness, the transitional state between wakefulness and sleep. Soon, I began to see in my mind's eye the figure of a woman's face, mostly in silhouette, the outline of which was undeniably my mother's. I could clearly see a 1950s hairstyle reminiscent of the bob worn by Queen Elizabeth II at the time, which my mother always wore. Inexplicably, I could feel her presence beside me.

No sooner had I realized this than I felt someone's hand softly brush my left ear, which was facing the ceiling. I knew it wasn't my wife, since she was on the other side of our bed sound asleep, her back faced toward mine, and the bed never moved. The touch was too heavy for a moth, for it made my ear move, but too light to be my son, for he was a clumsy teenager. The energetic presence and mysterious touch reminded me of my childhood experiences. I just stored this in my memory, not sure what to make of it. However, it raised my attention levels. I was certain there had to be more to come.

Sure enough, two weeks later I dreamed I was in my mother's New York City apartment, the one in which she lived after my father died. I stood in her living room facing a marble fireplace on the center of the far wall; Chinese porcelain dogs sat on either side of the marble hearth. The walls were painted yellow, and beautiful portraits hung around the room. A colonial-styled oval table with a white-and-blue needlepoint design lying underneath a glass top sat in the middle of the room in front of the fireplace. Underneath this table lay an ornate oriental rug, and two yellow love seats faced each other on either side of the table.

As I stood looking at the fireplace from across the living room, a yellow princess-style phone suddenly appeared in front of me. This style of phone from the 1970s (often referred to as a trimline corded wall-mountable phone), had tall, thin push buttons, and it was the identical phone my mother had installed in her kitchen. I watched as the index finger of a thin, boney hand with age spots began to slowly press each button on the phone. Every time the finger pressed a button, it held the button down for an inordinate period, as if trying to ensure that the button's signal was getting through. I could also hear the long tones emitted after the finger pressed each button.

This was unmistakably my mother's phone dialing method. I knew it well because her painfully slow dialing habits drove me crazy when she was alive. As I listened to what sounded like an emerging pattern, I thought it must be some new, unfamiliar type of Morse code done with push button phone sounds. In retrospect, I wonder if my mother was actually trying to communicate with me somehow using the phone's sounds or the letters represented on each button.

Finally I saw her full head in the lower part of my view. She stood there looking up at me with an uncertain, questioning look.

"I'm afraid," I heard my mother say without moving her lips.

I could see fear deep in her green eyes. This shocked me as my mother had always exuded self-confidence and certainty about everything. While alive in the physical, she carried this supreme confidence about anything she could see, feel, touch, or hear, and disregarded concepts that didn't fit her view of reality. In fact, after I'd begun speaking with my mother several years before she passed about my evolving views of the spirit world from everything I'd read, she got absolutely furious at me. When it came to intangible forces or God or the spirit world, despite her upbringing, she claimed herself a steadfast materialist, and no one was going to change her mind, least of all her own son.

Yet here she was, fifteen years after she passed, visiting me in my dream and admitting she was afraid. I paused as I wondered how could she still be afraid after all this time. I thought she would have learned a tremendous amount over the last fifteen years in the spirit world, so fear should be the last thing on her mind. Try as I might to rationalize the situation, the feeling that she needed *my* help rapidly grew.

At first I thought she was afraid of God's judgment. My mother had been raised in Ohio under the High Episcopal tradition, one similar to Catholicism. In her hidden belief system, God sat as both judge and jury, and rarely let people achieve the bliss of heaven, since everyone had sinned in some way. Yet this was fifteen years after she had passed into the spirit world, so wouldn't she have already faced judgment from her God? Then it dawned on me that my mother wasn't afraid of God's judgment. It was *my* judgment that terrified her.

My mother had been an alcoholic throughout my life. Ever since I could remember, about once a month she would go into her bedroom for several weeks like clockwork and rarely come out. When she did, she looked, sounded, and smelled like a completely different person. Her face was long and drawn, her eyes covered by drooping eyelids, her back bent low, her hair uncombed, her speech slurred, and her arms hanging low. Her entire personality was completely different, as if she was possessed by someone else. As a child I remember thinking that my mother had gone into a cave but a monster had come out. Needless to say, this caused me a great deal of distress in my youth. This also affected the rest of my life as I tried to deal with the subconscious trauma of my childhood.

So as I stood in front of my mother who had alerted me to her fear, I gave her the best advice I knew, some of which I'd picked up from reading and some from my guides.

"God loves you unconditionally, regardless of what you've ever done. He is love, and he'll always love you. Go into the light, for God is the light. I love you and always have. You did the best with what you had at the time. You did so much to raise me and prepare me for my life. Thank you for all your help. I love you."

The scene suddenly changed from my mother's apartment to a background of clouds. As if on cue, dark clouds above me began to part, and the sun's rays shone down onto the ground. My mother's face brightened and took on a warm glow from the sun. She smiled slightly and started to take on a more ethereal, misty form. Soon she drifted up above the clouds, and she was gone. I woke up with my eyes moist from tears.

The Final Dream Visitation

The final dream visitation appeared to represent a culmination of efforts by my family in spirit to alert me to their presence. It was early fall 2016, one month after my mother had visited me. I dreamed I stood in a late 1950s–early 1960s-style night club in New York City. I half expected Ricky Ricardo to appear and start singing "Babalau." Instead, my father appeared on the dance floor singing and dancing. He looked like he was in his forties, his skin tan, his white hair combed back, his physique lean. He wore neatly pressed white linen pants, new white espadrilles, and a short-sleeved button-down shirt that had thick black vertical stripes on a white background. He stepped forward to my right, and as he was about to perform, he turned to look at me and winked.

The unseen band changed its music to a soft, jazzy, cocktail lounge style. The crowd's voices mixed in as a dim background hum. Then my father stood in the middle of the dance floor as the club's lights were turned down low and a lone spotlight shown on him. He started singing a beautiful song with lyrics that seemed to repeat, "Nighty Night, na, na, Nighty Night, na, na, Nighty Night—"

He had a fantastic voice that amazed me, one that I never knew he had. In the middle of his routine, he moved over to a piano and continued the song while his fingers danced all over the keys creating gorgeous music. I was stunned. He almost seemed to be serenading someone. A crowd got up to encircle the dance floor, entranced by what they were seeing and hearing.

My mother walked out of the crowd, looking like she was in her forties, with her hair and clothing done in the 1950s style I'd seen in one of her earlier dream visitations. She walked to the center of the dance floor and waited. My father got up from his piano bench, walked over to her, and held out his hand. As the band played on, my mother took his hand in hers, and the two of them began to gracefully waltz together, each staring lovingly into the other's eyes, with broad smiles on their faces.

I stood there in shock. This was a side to my parents that I never knew existed. Never before had I seen them display loving emotions toward each other or exude such happiness; I'd never seen them dance together gracefully or exhibit such amazing musical talents. It made my heart swell to see my father looking so debonair and suave, and my mother so attracted to him. It looked like a scene from a romantic 1950s movie.

Something in the crowd off to my right caught my attention. I turned and scanned the circle of onlookers surrounding the dance floor. One person had stepped forward out of the crowd to stand closer to my parents. I quickly realized this was my mother's father—"Bampa" I'd called him as a child. He looked much younger than I remembered him from my childhood.

His face beamed with pride as he saw his daughter madly in love with this dashing and debonair young man. I felt like he was a proud father at his daughter's marriage. All I can recall from my few moments with Bampa as a child was a mean, old, abusive personality that I just didn't want to be near. Yet here he stood radiating love, happiness, and joy. He was a completely different person from the one I knew as a child. I awoke to realize that everyone had displayed themselves in their prime, and I saw sides to them I never knew existed.

The Visits Change

After making their impression on me during dream visitations, my family in spirit began contacting me when I was conscious—in my meditations. One weekend during the winter of 2016, I sat in my arm chair back in my man cave for an afternoon meditation. After focusing on my breathing for several minutes and relaxing in an effort to clear my mind, I invited spirit friends to step behind me and place their hands on my shoulders. I focused on my shoulders and tried to envision hands upon them.

Suddenly, I felt an immense tingling all around me, not just my upper arms. I immediately sensed my mother's presence. *Somehow, I knew she stood right in front of me.* I'm not sure how I knew it was her, other than a deep-seated *knowing*—that feeling you get deep in your solar plexus that leaves you without a doubt in your mind.

A bubble of love and warmth enveloped me, as if my mother had thrown her arms around me in a giant, loving hug. I silently asked her to put her hands in mine. As I did, my hands grew warmer. I felt another energy on them, resting gently on top.

"I love you, Mom," I said out loud, hoping I'd get a response.

Then I felt her energy move closer to me and touch my knees, my legs, my chest, and my head. Every part of my body felt like electricity was coursing through it as the tingling grew in intensity. By this point, I had uncontrollable tears of joy streaming down my face as I was overcome with emotion and the intensity of reunion. Finally, after fifteen years I consciously reconnected with my mother with whom I'd felt separated by physical death. This was the same feeling I'd experienced when my father and I had embraced in my dream earlier in the year. While this was a beautiful interaction with my spirit family, they weren't finished yet.

That same week I again sat in meditation, but this time I travelled back to the towering emerald structure with gigantic pointy spires, which stood on the hill. As I admired the building, my entire body tingled with the effervescent, champagne-like energy. I found myself inside once again, standing in the center hall. To my left I saw countless book shelves soaring hundreds of stories into the air, each packed with every conceivable type of book. Brilliant white light streamed down onto the white marble floor of the center hallway and seemed to bounce around every corner of the interior, providing light everywhere.

In front of me on the first floor across the main entrance hall, I saw the large oak door with a shiny brass handle. It had the same sign on the door that read Meeting In Progress. I walked over to the door and opened it with confidence. There in front of me lay the huge oval table made out of marble that I'd seen before, surrounded by the same eight empty, ornately carved wooden chairs. Where were my spirit guides?

Off to the left side of the table, I saw many of my family members who had previously passed away standing there smiling at me. They come up to me and hugged me in what truly felt like a homecoming. Before me stood both my parents, my grandparents who had recently visited me in my dreams, and my aunt and uncle from my father's side of the family. As they all hugged me, I felt their unconditional love and support. I saw my mother's warm smile and my father's pride and joy as he smiled from ear to ear. Everyone was so happy.

I started to feel that higher powers were trying to reach out to me, as if to say, "Wake up." At that point, I realized something within me was beginning to irrevocably change, and I knew I had an obligation to explore what was occurring and fully understand it.

3

Further Exploration

"In wisdom gathered over time I have found that every experience is a form of exploration."
—Ansel Adams

After my experiences, I realized that somehow my awakening "turned on" a previously suppressed ability to communicate with spirit and was meant to be shared with others and used for love. Once I came to grips with what was happening, I focused my efforts more on communication, whether that was during a meditation, a dream, or a different approach. I ran across a communication method I hadn't tried previously that appeared a bit easier as I learned that people without mediumistic abilities were able to interact with spirit.

Automatic Writing

I tried automatic writing as a new way to contact my guides. Automatic writing is the process of writing material that does not come from the conscious mind. While the writer may hold the pen, he or she may not be aware of what is written by his spirit communicator. On one occasion I had a rather unusual experience that helped me expand my communication ability. I sat down at my desk one morning and began silently asking my guides for their help and advice about what was happening in my life and what my mission was. This is a transcription of my short contact:

Q: I want to speak with my loving spirit guides.

(long pause)

A: Speak … we shall be heard.

Q: What is your name?

A: Rebecca.* I love you forever. Know this. I am with you always.

Q: Rebecca, what is my purpose here?

A: To learn and grow.

Q: What am I supposed to learn?

A: How to learn to love.

Q: What is the afterlife like?

A: Beautiful, but it is your creation. I am the now and forever … You are on your path.

Q: How do I grow my soul?

A: Through love. All that you read now and experience now is real. Do not doubt your own mind. Know you are loved always and forever. Be compassionate. I will help you listen to yourself. Speak with Victoria and gain knowledge. 1886.

**note: I felt like I wanted to write Rebecca Solomon*

Needless to say, I was rather stunned by what came out of that contact attempt. I had no idea who Victoria was nor what the number 1886 meant. I guessed that it might be the year she died, or perhaps when Rebecca died, but I couldn't be sure. I thought this was so interesting that a few days later I sat for another automatic writing session.

Sitting at my desk one weekend morning, I closed my eyes so I could concentrate on reaching spirit. I let my eyelids stay barely open so I could see the paper and not make a mess. At first nothing happened, so I felt a bit let down. But suddenly, it felt like someone jumped inside my head and was trying to get my attention. I doubled my focus on what was happening. Then I just wanted to write words as fast as I could and get my torrent of thoughts out on paper. This is what came out:

Dear One: Your growing love is helping you evolve. More love comes from within and is shared with others. To evolve, you must share your growing love and understanding with those around you. Think of it as the Christ Light emanating from within you trying to get out. Add light to the darkness of those around you so they can see the truth. You too can be the beacon to illuminate the path. But, like all fires that burn and shine brightly, it takes energy to shine this light, and it needs a loving spark and lots of energy to sustain.

I was amazed by what I read and the numerous subtle meanings. Encouraged, I tried a few other contacts using automatic writing, but they came out too messy for me to understand them.

Closer Contact

I moved back to trying to contact spirit again during my meditation sessions. One particular meditation caught my attention as it began to strongly combine visual imagery with tingling sensations and overpowering feelings of love. This went beyond earlier spirit guide images and bordered on the perception of an angelic being. Just remember, however, that I still didn't believe in angels, so this experience really knocked my socks off.

As usual, I was sitting in my armchair listening to soft meditation music and just beginning to feel more relaxed. I kept my eyes closed, as I felt this could allow my mind to go where it needed without distraction. After sitting comfortably in my chair for a while, I noticed that my mind started to become quite focused and active. It felt like some energy was trying to enter or merge with my consciousness.

The experience began with a view of an endless dark background. Soon, I began to see a small, fuzzy pinpoint of light far off in the distance that was slowly growing as it approached. The object started to take on a more silvery, reflective appearance, and its shape changed from a round white orb to a thin vertical sliver of light with gentle shapes coming out from its sides. As it got still closer, I could see more details and saw the object became a flowing, ornate white robe. The robe seemed foggy, but also brilliantly white as if it was bursting with energy and electricity.

At first, I couldn't tell if the figure wearing the robe was male or female, but as more details continued to fill in, I saw the person was a slender young woman with very dark, almost jet-black, hair. She had beautiful, long flowing hair falling down her back to her hips in graceful waves that reminded me of a horse's mane. She had a tiny porcelain white face and a small head that seemed almost too small for her body. The woman appeared to be young, in her late twenties. Her eyes sparkled an amazing mix of brilliant violet, purple, and indigo, together with a deep blue, yet they were all one color. I'd never seen any color on earth quite like this before. As I stared at the woman's eyes, they just seemed too large for her face. It dawned on me that this was the same woman I'd seen in a previous meditation.

Her body appeared to float six to twelve inches off the ground, and the bottom of her robe just seemed to fade away. As I scanned her robe again, I noticed a soft white mist or glow surrounding it that extended out a foot or two. Her entire robe billowed softly as if it were being blown gently in a soft breeze. What appeared to be a tall collar stood up high in the back. The more I looked, the more I realized this wasn't just a collar, but something that emanated from the woman's back, reminding me of wings that stood higher than the top of a head. I was captivated by what I saw.

I asked the woman to stand behind me and wrap herself around me like a blanket. Soon, a warm wave of energy along with a tingling sensation overwhelmed every inch of my body. This loving energy regenerated me, brought peace to my mind, lifted my spirits, and opened my awareness to a greater existence. The universe reached out its arms, embraced me, and shared its expansive and unconditional love because I existed. I sat in this state of bliss absorbing every morsel of affection I could and thought that time stood still.

The declining intensity and vibration levels of the energy announced its slow retreat as I saw the woman begin to pull back and shrink as she got farther away. I had to sit in my armchair staring into space for several minutes just to come back to a fully conscious state and take note of what I'd just experienced. I had no definite idea about what I'd just seen, whom I'd met or what the being was.

In my mind I was more comfortable with the woman existing as a plain old spirit guide, but I started to think that I might have had an encounter with something higher than that. I felt reluctant to admit the woman might be an angel, despite my previous awakening. To me that smacked of religion, and I still distrusted religious concepts. Nevertheless, I had to acknowledge that something extraordinary had happened, and this forced me to reexamine all my old beliefs.

That wasn't the only time I encountered an angelic being, though at the time I don't think I referred to them as such. During one meditation when I was particularly upset and depressed about certain events occurring in my life, I just sat and tried to center myself. I silently and slowly repeated the phrase, "I am Love," though I certainly didn't feel it. I kept doing this, but I thought I was just trying to fool myself. Out of the blue, I saw a beautiful, angelic being in my mind. She approached as a soft, tingling energy pressed down on the skin around my hand. She had very light skin on her face, though under her eyes it appeared quite pink. She wore a garland of yellow daisies atop her head, and her hair was long, brown, and quite curly. I thought this angelic figure was too good to be true, but I went along for the ride.

We began to float up toward a bright light above us, though I didn't know or see the source. We rested partway along our journey for a while because dark clouds hung over us and, inexplicably, wouldn't let us pass. Suddenly, a huge hole opened above us, and bright rays of golden-white light streamed around me in a wide array. The light was almost blinding, and so intense that I had to cover my eyes with my hands and squint. As the familiar tingling sensation spread from my hand to touch every part of me, I realized I was in contact with spiritual energy again. Then the intense light shining all around me grew even brighter. I sensed I was in the presence of something *far* greater than myself. I wasn't sure if it was something divine or not, but it made a lasting impression on me. At the end of the session, I realized I'd been touched by pure love and compassion.

Looking back on these encounters, I occasionally think my guides were practically hitting me over the head with a cane to wake me up. It's clear they were trying to get me to accept that not only were they real, but higher beings including angels and the Divine were not merely figments of my imagination. One particular episode comes to mind that represents a culmination of their efforts.

In another meditation, I was again chanting mantras in an effort to help me focus. I mentally recited, "I am love, I am forgiveness." After repeating that for some time, I added in front of those phrases the mantra, "I am spirit, I am light." Then I just repeated that four phrase mantra for probably ten minutes. I didn't really expect anything to happen, just a heightened sense of focus. However, I experienced a profound journey similar to my awakening, and it finally convinced me I wasn't imagining everything.

Without realizing it, I had shortened my mantra to "I Am," the same phrase relating to God that appears over 300 times in the Bible. Soon, everything around me just began to fade away as I started feeling united with Source energy. I felt I was everywhere and nowhere at the same time. The space around me was infinite and bright white. There was no beginning and no ending, but I was at the center of an infinite sphere. Sheer euphoria and ecstasy overwhelmed me, and I didn't want to go back. No sooner did that thought cross my mind than I became aware of my body again so I knew I was still connected to the earth, but my mind was in another dimension. I realized I was spirit and my dense, physical being was an illusion, not the other way around. I yearned for the euphoric feeling of spirit to return.

After having those numerous experiences, I sensed I began to change from within. I experienced everything with more emotion as my sensitivity and empathy started to increase. I would get choked up and teary eyed during emotional movies and plays. I just wanted to let my tears run free and bawl and just let all my feelings out, though I tried my best to hide it from friends and family. After all, I thought to myself, men don't cry.

Sometimes, I thought I was getting more emotional than the women around me and felt like a sap. I learned, however, that I was beginning to get in touch with the feminine side of my brain, which allowed my empathic abilities to grow. When I would read books or watch performances by mediums, for example, I could viscerally feel a sharp tugging at my heart strings. I observed dramatic healing taking place when a recipient heard from their loved ones with indisputable, evidential information. Despite my previous self-centered and male-dominated existence, I sensed a growing need to help and heal others, though I had no idea why or from where it came.

During this time of transition, I witnessed mediumship

readings for parents who had lost the will to live after their children had passed into spirit. Once they were reunited with their children, however, they found the spark to carry on. Husbands or wives who had lost their spouses felt incomplete without their other half. Yet when their loved ones came through with their unique information and messages, the sitters' entire demeanor and outlook on life dramatically improved. In short, the transformations that occurred were nothing short of miraculous and brought about by love.

That's when it hit me. I wanted to do exactly the same thing. I wanted to bring hope where there was only despair, bring love where there was only emptiness, and bring light where there was only darkness. I wanted to heal and comfort people who were searching for how to carry on with their lives after the death of a loved one. I wanted to help transform people's lives and bring through the power of spirit's love. I wanted to show those in mourning that death is not the end, but that life does continue and that our loved ones remain with us. In short, I wanted to be a medium.

Ever since that fateful morning when those four spirits appeared before me, I've become more involved with spirit and have continued learning how to communicate with them; this is a journey that will never end. Spirit always amazes me in readings with their intelligence, ingenuity, and creativity for turning symbolic images, thoughts, songs, or feelings into clear and meaningful evidential information and messages. Every day I look forward to what spirit will do to bring through proof of survival and what healing messages they bring to their loved ones here on earth. For me, the journey continues each day.

Now that I'm a medium, I've been blessed to watch the

incredible transformations brought about by spirit. I'm honored just to be a part of it. I've witnessed firsthand how grown children reconnect with their parents in spirit who hadn't physically seen their grandchildren grow up. I've helped people reunite with their best friends like they were close siblings. I've enabled people to hear from their parents again after a tragic or upsetting passing. I've reunited spouses or siblings who miss each other terribly, but whose bonds of love keep them together. There is absolutely no doubt in my mind that the loving and transformative power of spirit has healed all of my clients. So much love comes through in these sessions, that I find myself transformed and healed as a result. Perhaps that's another reason why I became a medium. Spirit's love can heal us all, regardless of our part in the conversation—even when we don't expect it.

4

Death Is Not Goodbye

"Just when the caterpillar thought its life was over, it became a butterfly."
—Proverb

My father died when I was just eighteen and probably needed him the most, although I'm sure I never admitted it then, for I was a rebellious and fiercely independent teenager. I was certain I'd never see him again. His death turned my world upside down, and it caused a huge piece of me to die inside. I kept thinking, "How can I go on? Why did he leave me here? What did I do to deserve this? My world will never be the same. I feel so alone, and no one could possibly understand my horrible grief."

These were just some of the endless thoughts flying through my brain at the time. I was convinced my life as I knew it was over and that my father had left me here on this lonely, desolate earth to fend for myself. Even though my mother was still alive, it felt like everyone had died. In fact, soon thereafter my mother, aunt, and uncle did go to join my father and grandparents, so I *was* alone. I felt deserted by my family until three decades later when I actually saw and spoke to my father clear as day, and I began having clear conversations with other family members soon after. That was when my reality dramatically changed forever.

Many people who lose a loved one feel as if they will never see or hear from that person again and feel that this life in the physical is everything we have. Most of us grow up believing this reality is all we have, for we intimately experience it with our five physical senses. A large number of people still believe we live one life on this earth and that's the end of our lives. They think we just become food for the worms. While the loss of life on earth is most assuredly something that produces real grief, the passing must be seen in perspective.

There is a vast amount of evidence, both anecdotal and scientific, clearly displaying that our life continues beyond the physical, just not where we can see it with our human eyes. As this mountain of evidence grows, so too does the number of people who realize that life after physical death is real. According to the International Association for Near-Death Studies, well over 5 percent of the global population—over 400 million people—have had a near-death experience (NDE). As these people return from their experiences and describe what they have seen (which often defies logical explanation), we are coming to understand what happens after the physical body dies. The transition called "death" is really just a metamorphosis whereby our "being" evolves into another state with our consciousness intact. Our loved ones are still with us in another form; we just can't see them.

Energy—A Little Science Lesson

Our fundamental perception and perspective often lead us to inaccurate conclusions. Science, especially quantum mechanics, has proven that we and everything around us are just energy. Electrons, neutrons, protons, and quarks are all just subatomic particles of energy vibrating at extremely high speeds. When you look at objects at a microscopic scale you discover that everything consists of empty space with small particles floating adrift, but all highly energized. It is a microscopic view of what the universe looks like: just vast, empty space with energy at its core.

Although you perceive the chair you're sitting on as solid, it only feels solid because extraordinary energy is required to push together the atoms of the chair (and the atoms of your body)—more than we can exert. We feel this as resistance and therefore believe that objects are solid. But quantum physics states that matter accounts for only 28 percent of everything that exists, while the remaining 72 percent represents pure energy.

Energy can be measured in wavelengths, frequencies, and oscillations, as can molecules, color, and sound. In a similar vein, a vibration rate is the speed of oscillation, or the speed at which something moves back and forth. At the atomic level, vibration can be understood to be the speed at which electrons orbit the nucleus of the atom.

The best example of energy as a vibration is a propeller or a fan blade. When at rest, the blade can easily be seen since it is oscillating at a rate of zero. However, at a high enough speed, the blade seems to disappear before our eyes. Is the blade gone? No, it's still there, but it's just at a higher rate of vibration, one that we can't see. The same could be said of subatomic particles; if we were to view them with a powerful electron microscope, they could be easily seen at rest; at their high vibration state, however, they seem to be invisible because they're moving so fast around the nucleus.

Another example is the different states of matter (solid, liquid, gas), all dependent on the vibration rates of the particles. Ice, for example, is solid water that is extremely dense (particles are tightly packed together) with its atoms hardly moving at all amid very low kinetic energy. Ice is solid and easily seen, just like the dense matter of the human body. Increase the level of energy (meaning the temperature), and the solid water becomes a liquid as its molecules become more excited and vibrate at a higher rate. Raise the energy level further still and the liquid water becomes a gas, that is, steam. In this state, the particles have a great deal of space between them and have high kinetic energy; they are vibrating at an even faster rate. This gaseous state is difficult to see with the human eye (think of air) and similar to spirit, which vibrates at an even higher rate.

An additional example is sound and the different hearing ranges between humans and dogs. Sound is nothing but air waves oscillating at different vibrations. Humans can detect sounds up to a maximum of 23,000 Hz, while dogs typically can detect sounds above those of humans (up to 45,000 Hz). Just because we can't hear the sounds that dogs can hear, does that mean those sounds aren't there? No, the sounds are still there, but they are oscillating at higher vibrations, and we can't detect them.

Likewise, consider light wavelengths. Lizards can see in the ultraviolet spectrum (10nm-400nm) unlike humans that are limited to only visible light (400-700 nm). Does that mean that because we can't see it with the naked eye, ultraviolet light doesn't exist? No, it just means that its vibrating at a different wavelength and we can't easily see it.

In his theory for the Law of Conservation of Mass Energy, Albert Einstein wrote, "Energy cannot be created or destroyed, it can only be changed from one form to another." *We are energy, nothing more,* vibrating at a specific frequency on earth that's slow enough we can see it. Speed up that vibration to hyper speeds, however, and something magical happens. While the material, chemically produced electrical energy in our bodies may dissipate, our higher vibration spirit energy, also known as our consciousness, leaves behind the slower vibration material existence.

Though traditional science under the laws of the Newtonian world remains steadfast in its notion that the conscious mind exists within the brain, quantum mechanics suggests it resides there only temporarily. According to the theory of quantum entanglement, or what Einstein called, "spooky action at a distance," electrons can move instantaneously from point A to point B without passing through intermediate points over space and time, without energy exchange, as if they were already there. This gives rise to the theory that an object can be nonlocal in space and time. In other words, it can exist in more than one place at one time, omnipresent, infinite in time. Under this theory, consciousness is not limited to the physical brain and time is not linear, as Einstein displayed in his general theory of relativity.

Spirit Is Energy

Spirit is actually energy vibrating at a higher rate than what we can sense with our five physical senses. Just because we can't readily sense something doesn't mean it doesn't exist. We all have energy bodies and well-defined energy systems and centers, including bioenergetic systems and the body's electrical system, something well known to modern medical science.

The electrical energy in our brain, for example, can be measured by an EEG (electroencephalogram) that measures the electrical charges in our brain cells. We also have the body's meridian system and energy centers known by Eastern medicine for thousands of years. These are defined by seven main chakras, translated from the Hindu Vedas as wheels of energy. In fact, energy is the basis for energy healing such as Reiki, which has existed for thousands of years. The Chinese word for energy is chi, as in tai chi, while the Japanese word for energy is ki, as in Reiki.

When the physical body dies, the energy it once contained has to go somewhere because the energy can't be destroyed (remember Einstein). While the electrochemical energy dissipates, the spirit energy is released from its vessel, the brain. This energy has been measured with sensitive EMF (Electro Magnetic Frequency) devices that measure fluctuations in electromagnetic fields. Spirit energy has been seen countless times leaving the human body at the time of physical death in hospices and hospitals by physicians, caregivers, and family.

Our consciousness is the intelligent aspect of our energy, and this is what remains alive after death, for this is energy that exists beyond the material state. There are so many reports of the consciousness remaining alive after death, including NDEs, reincarnation, communication with spirit, automatic writing, and more, that if were they stacked one on top of another, they would soar miles above the earth.

There are countless mediums throughout the world who have highly developed their mediumistic senses (the five "clairs," which I'll detail in Chapter 5). As a result, they can detect spirit's higher vibrations exceedingly well, make clear contact with spirit, and bring forth highly detailed evidential information. Everyone has the ability to detect spirit—it's just a matter of developing one's sense enough. We all have intuition, for example, that "gut feeling," and we rely on this regularly. We all can detect or feel people's moods or the mood of a room if we allow ourselves to be open. These are common psychic abilities that everyone has.

Quantum mechanics states that all living beings are created from the same material as the quantum vacuum, or zero point, essentially a heaving sea of vibrating energy. Living beings are composed of packets of quantum energy that continually exchange information with the vacuum. Consequently, not only do we live in the universe, but the universe lives in us—we are interconnected. As eminent Harvard psychiatrist William James wrote in 1902, "There is a continuum of cosmic consciousness ... into which our several minds plunge as into a mother-sea or reservoir."[2]

Why is it so difficult to believe that the ultimate transformation from physical to nonphysical and visible to invisible with full consciousness is very real? As Jesuit priest Pierre Teilhard de Chardin has been quoted, "We are not human beings having a spiritual experience, we are spiritual beings have a human experience." It is clear that our best selves remain alive after our physical passing and leave behind the ego. Consequently, spirit is full of love and seeks to pass on loving, healing messages to those in need.

Bridging the Gap

We all know someone who has lost a loved one, or perhaps we may have lost one or more loved ones ourselves. Grief in these situations is painful; it may last for years, and it is personal and individual with no two experiences being the same. Grief is nonlinear and includes both recovery and setbacks. Complex emotions explode into the open and may intensify the grief we feel. These emotions, which typically include shock, denial, anger, guilt, yearning, confusion, feelings of powerlessness, and a loss of hope, are all perfectly normal. In some cases, the bereaved loses the will to carry on or the desire to live life to the fullest and becomes a mere shell of their former self.

However, while we in the physical ache for the return of our lost loved one, their spirit is very much alive, just not where we can typically sense it. This may appear to be little consolation to the bereaved and may seem to be just a mere platitude. Yet consider the countless times spirit has come through to their families (either individually to them or through evidential mediums), given incontrovertible evidence of their continued existence, and provided an overwhelming sense of joy and relief to the bereaved. This is pure love coming through from the spirit world.

What could possibly constitute incontrovertible evidence and be so compelling that it would convince even the most skeptical among us that spirits are quite alive and still sending us their love? A good start is when the evidential medium only provides unusually detailed information that they could not have gotten from anywhere but spirit without asking questions, can do so with a high level of accuracy, and that the client can confirm.

Important evidential information that spirit will provide goes beyond general descriptions like gender, age at passing and cause of death (though that's a beginning). Compelling descriptions include the loved ones' unique physical features, personality, character traits, unique identifications or markings, speech patterns, unusual mannerisms, hobbies, habits, words or phrases unique to them, and special items of significance to loved ones here on earth. Additional items include their history growing up, their background, their marital status, and their personal preferences. Again, all this is provided without questioning or any information in advance (sitters take note).

Some of the *most* convincing evidence spirit provides us includes shared memories, descriptions of events that happened *after* they passed, descriptions of occurrences that only the sitter knows about, approval of decisions we have made without them in the physical, and other family members who are with them in spirit. After all this evidence, spirit then gives us their loving messages of healing and comfort. Though we may be in such a deep state of grief that we feel we can't go on, spirit is urging us to live our lives to the fullest.

Spirit is just pure energy, the true survival of consciousness in the nonphysical. It's like the oft-cited example of how we think of ourselves internally through the aging process. As we age, we continue to think of the "me" inside us as being the same regardless of whether we are ten or 110. Our consciousness remains the same, for it's the one constant. The only thing that changes is our physical body. While our physical body may age and die, our consciousness remains very much alive, just without the ego attached. Thus, when a spirit comes through in a reading, their personality remains the same and is immediately recognizable to their family. What messages get sent the loudest? They are the messages of their unconditional love for us and the unconditional love they received when they transformed into spirit.

While it may seem unfair that our loved one has passed on, just remember they are still with us and alive in spirit, can hear our thoughts, and are always sending us loving thoughts to us … even if we can't hear them with our ears. People often lament how desperately they miss their loved ones, which is perfectly understandable and is a normal human reaction. However, I have come to discover that when our loved ones leave their earthly body, they never really leave us. They have just transformed from a state of physical existence to a state of nonphysical existence. The energy form that existed previously, the consciousness, is very much alive, as energy cannot be created or destroyed; it can only change form.

I often compare this to the transformation that occurs when a caterpillar becomes a butterfly. Did the caterpillar die? No, it just shed its cocoon and changed form to become a gorgeous insect with wings. This is similar to what happens when we humans shed our earthly bodies. We are vibrant spirit energy temporarily housed in human bodies that has come to learn specific lessons in the earth school. We often search for greater meaning and ask, "Why am I here?" That would be like asking the teacher for the answers on the test in the lesson you were studying. If you knew the answers, how could you learn?

Once we have learned our lessons here on earth and our spiritual mission has been accomplished, our higher self determines it is time to return home to our spirit family. At this point, the astral body or etheric double finally disconnects from the several chakra points that held it to the human body and evolves into a more rarified form to merge with its spiritual family. Upon being greeted by its loved ones in spirit, the newly arrived spirit receives a warm and loving homecoming reception, much like a party or family parade.

If its departure from earth was sudden or unexpected, such as in an accident, then the new spirit may be taken by its guides to the equivalent of a rest home or hospital for recovery and rest. Everyone in the spirit world is well aware of the scheduled arrival of the new spirit and treats him or her with vast amounts of love. All spirits, once they have acclimated to their new world, are still aware of their family back on earth, for it is the love that connects them and that is heightened when they reach the spirit world.

In readings with my clients, it is this love that comes through so strongly for sitters left behind. First, spirit wants to make sure the sitter clearly understands and fully believes they in fact are hearing from their dearly departed loved one. As a result, they provide tremendous amounts of evidential information that only they and the sitter could know, to prove their afterlife existence to the sitter. Once the relationship has been clearly established, they send their message of love, forgiveness, or apology to the sitter. Forgiveness and apology often comes out in a reading, since spirit has its life review and sees for itself how it could have lived a better life. We judge ourselves more harshly than any other person ever could.

Make no mistake, spirit is not up in heaven just playing

with harps. They are quite active improving themselves and learning many things, especially since they have no limitations or ego anymore. Spirit is also following what we do here on earth. They can hear our thoughts, see what we do and how we live our lives. They only want what is best for us. Quite often they are trying to pass messages to us, but we just don't hear them or detect them. We may sense them in dreams, though even those can be fleeting.

Examples of spirit trying to get our attention include getting an unexpected idea in our head out of the blue, getting a gut feeling in our stomach (intuition), hearing our name or a sound when there is no one else around, electronics acting unusually for no apparent reason, getting a tingling feeling or sensing someone is nearby but not seeing anyone, seeing a flash or image out of the corner of your eye but having it disappear when you turn to look at it, or objects falling over or moving by themselves without a rational explanation. These are just some of the typical ways spirit tries to catch our attention.

Unfortunately, most people ignore their surroundings and walk around feeling that anything that happens to them is attributable only their physical bodies or minds and nothing more. The majority of us have difficulty believing that there is anything beyond this life, and many don't know their purpose for being here in the first place. We often encounter difficulties because we're so focused on ourselves and this life that we can't see the bigger picture. But what if we had a different perspective?

Our experience seems limited by our view of our world and can be summarized by the saying "You see what you believe." In Plato's *Allegory of the Cave,* for example, three prisoners have lived their lives chained to a cave wall, facing it. They watch shadows projected onto that wall from objects passing in front of a fire behind them and see the shadows as real people. These shadow people become their reality, for they know nothing else. One prisoner escapes from the cave, goes outside, and learns that his previous reality was not reality at all. When he returns to inform the other prisoners about the true nature of reality that he has seen, they refuse to accept it, for this is beyond their comprehension and everything they know about their world.

Plato had great insight, for this allegory fits perfectly with our view of reality on earth. Most of us prisoners on earth see the physical universe as the true reality, for we have known nothing else. Yet the countless communications with spirit who have returned to describe a dramatically different existence than one we're used to demonstrates a greater reality we need to acknowledge. Furthermore, these well-documented and endless interactions show proof of survival of consciousness and the broader reality of our souls.

Many people see our bodies as the dominant being and think of it in terms of the primary outer circle, with our soul as our energy or small inner circle. They look on our spirit as our spark and tiny inside circle. Yet the reality is in fact reversed. Our spirit is our dominant being, pictured as our primary and controlling outer circle. This is followed by our soul, or smaller inner circle, and finally our physical body, which is a tiny aspect of our being compared to our broader, all-encompassing spirit. We need to see ourselves as larger spirit beings housing physical bodies within.

As spirit has described, we return to physical existence from the spiritual realm so we can learn new lessons that will help our spiritual growth. The difficulties we experience in the physical are more challenging than in the spirit world, and consequently we gain greater insight and learn faster than we might otherwise. We cycle through the physical many times, and our larger existence is in the nonphysical reality.

If we consider ourselves spiritual beings, then we realize we are capable of so much more. We can love more freely, forgive more readily, act more compassionately, interact more harmoniously, and bring peace to our reality, all the while fueling our spiritual growth. If we change our reality to understand that we are spiritual beings having a human experience, then we transcend our physical limitations and broaden our capabilities. See yourself as spirit and expand. Never again think that spirit has left you or is not around, for spirit is always around you sending love.

5

The Human Subtle Energy System

"Spiritual energy is the one kind that never runs out."
—Deepak Chopra

I chose to add this chapter as a way to help explain how we humans are just beings of energy. This material may get a bit esoteric, but I feel it's important to understand. While we may look at our physical body and think we extend out only to our skin, in fact our body as defined by our energy field, or aura, extends far beyond what we can see with our physical eyes. Photos of auras have been captured using Kirlian photography, which uses high voltage metal plates, showing the energy system extending up to several feet. The physical body is just the center of multiple layers of subtle energies that exist at different vibrations or frequencies. Each layer of the energy field connects to the physical body through the chakras, which are spinning vortexes that draw in energy. In case you aren't familiar with chakras and the energy bodies as they are described in ancient texts, I'll briefly summarize them.

This subtle, dynamic energy system of our body facilitates our consciousness and rules our ability to think, feel emotions, participate in activities, and make memories. In fact, these energy bodies facilitate spiritual growth and transcendence to higher levels of consciousness. As a result of our subtle energy bodies, we truly exist as spirit, both while in the physical and while in the nonphysical. In fact, as we pass into spirit, our energy body releases the physical body like a snake sheds old skin.

The Chakras

The word *chakra* originates from an ancient Sanskrit word meaning *wheel of light*. The chakra system originated in India between 1500 and 500 BCE in the oldest text called the Vedas, and later in the Upanishads, which are some of the most authoritative Hindu texts. In Hinduism and Buddhism a chakra is defined as a nonphysical energy center of power. Chakra centers are situated where the crossing points of energy channels called *nadis* meet. Nadis are the conduits in the subtle body through which the life force, or prana, circulates.

The chakras, aligned with our spine, are linked to different parts of the body and its functions from mental to physical to spiritual. Importantly, chakras act as a conduit for the energy to flow through the body. The primary chakra system within the body consists of seven main energy centers, or spinning vortexes of energy. They act as energy gateways or energy exchange points between their related subtle energy bodies and the physical body via the meridian system, which is responsible for energy distribution. They have a significant impact on our aura, or energy field, and our overall health and well-being. This is the basis for energy healing, including Reiki, spiritual healing and other modalities, which is a topic for another book by itself.

The Root Chakra

The first chakra is the root chakra or *muladhara*, located at the perineum, or the base of the spine. Its color is red, and its element is the earth. As it is closest to the earth, its function is associated with earthly grounding, security, and physical survival. It controls your fight or flight response. For bodily functions, this chakra is associated with the legs, feet, bones, large intestine, and adrenal glands. When this chakra is open you feel stable, secure, and grounded. If you feel fearful or nervous, your root chakra may be underactive. Conversely, if you're obsessed with security, resist change, or are very materialistic and greedy, then this chakra may be overactive.

The Sacral Chakra

The second main chakra is the sacral chakra or *svadhisthana*, which is located near your pubic bone. Its color is orange, while its element is water. This chakra is related to sensuality, sexuality, the desire for pleasure and feeling. It is associated with the reproductive organs, bladder, spleen, kidneys, and the legs. It represents the "liquids" of the body, meaning blood circulation, urine production and elimination, and sexual body fluids. When this chakra is open, your feelings flow freely; you are open to intimacy and are passionate. If this is overactive, you can be manipulative, controlling, lustful, and addictive.

When this is closed, you tend to be stiff, unemotional, and not very open to people. At worst, you can be codependent, a martyr, and submissive, and you don't feel anything.

The Solar Plexus Chakra

The third primary chakra is the solar plexus chakra or *manipura,* located near your diaphram. Its color is yellow, and its element is fire. This chakra is related to will-power, motivation, assertiveness, joy, vitality and your desire to express your own individuality. It governs the ability to judge, form opinions and create thoughts. Similar to the meridian system, this chakra is responsible for energy distribution and the regulation of metabolic energy throughout the body. Regarding bodily functions, it is associated with the pancreas, stomach, liver and gall-bladder. When this is open, you feel in control with good self-esteem. When this chakra is underactive, you may feel timid, disliked and indecisive. However, if it is overactive, you may be egotistical, domineering and possibly overly aggressive.

The Heart Chakra

The fourth chakra is the heart chakra or *anahata,* located in the center of the chest, which is associated with the color green. Its element is air. This is the center of true love, compassion, and spiritual growth. It is the bridge that connects the lower physical chakras and the upper spiritual chakras, as well as our lower and higher energies of our being. This chakra is associated with the heart, liver, lungs, thymus gland, the immune system, and blood circulation. When this chakra is open, you are compassionate, loving, and kind. If this is overactive, you may suffocate people with your love (possibly for selfish reasons) and may have poor emotional boundaries. When this is underactive, however, you may be heartless, ruthless, cold, and distant.

The Throat Chakra

The fifth chakra is the throat chakra or *vishuddha*. This is located in the throat and associated with the color light-blue. Its element is sound. This chakra is the center of communication, self-expression, and creativity. The throat chakra is associated with the thyroid gland, throat, upper lungs, arms, and digestive tract. When this is underactive you may be introverted, shy, quiet, unable to creatively express yourself, or may lack faith. Conversely, if this is overactive, you may be willful, controlling, or judgmental, have hurtful speech, speak too much, or be a bad listener.

The Third Eye Chakra

The sixth main chakra is the third eye chakra or *ajna*, which is located on the middle of the forehead about an inch above the eyebrows. Its color is indigo, and its element is light. This is the home of intuition, spiritual vision, insight, and "the mind's eye." This chakra is associated with perception, knowingness, wisdom, imagination, and self-mastery. This chakra is also related to clairvoyance, intuition, and visualization, and it governs spirituality and the inherent need in humans to search for the meaning of life. The third eye chakra is associated with the pineal and pituitary glands, lower brain, left eye, nose, and the ears. The opening of the third eye corresponds with spiritual awakening. If this is underactive, you may not be very good at thinking for yourself, tend to rely on set beliefs too much, have unclear thought, or be deluded and may be rigid in your thinking. If this is overactive, however, you may be overly analytical or intellectual.

The Crown Chakra

The seventh chakra is the crown chakra or *sahasrara,* located at the top or crown of the head. Its color is violet, while its element is thought. This is connected to spirituality and self-enlightenment. The Hopi word for the crown chakra, *kopavi,* means "open door" or "open window."[3] This chakra enables unification of the higher self with the human personality. It is associated with spiritual will, inspiration, unity, divine wisdom and understanding, idealism, selfless service, perception beyond space and time, and the continuity of consciousness. The crown chakra is associated with the pineal gland, cerebral cortex, central nervous system, and the right eye. Blockages will result in negativity, loneliness, depression, nightmares, confusion, lack of inspiration, alienation, and hesitation to serve.

The Energy Bodies

Our aura, or energy field, is an electromagnetic field that emanates from and surrounds our physical body. The aura is composed of seven primary energy bodies that each represent a level of energy and correspond with a specific primary chakra. As an energy field, our aura is always on, whether we are aware of it or not. For example, when we meet someone for the first time or shake their hand, we instantly have a feeling about the other person, however subtle that feeling might be. We could feel an immediate liking and attraction to or an immediate discomfort with that person. These feelings represent our auric energy field interacting with the other person's auric field and sensing their energy—positive or negative.

Each of our energy bodies, which together, compose our aura, are like concentric layers (one within the other) that inter-penetrate each other due to the unique vibrational frequency of each. The first three layers are related to the physical body, the second three layers are related to the spiritual body, and the last layer is the connection with the Divine Source. While each body is layered on top of one another, each one also includes each of the layers below it, such that layer 7 is also part of layer 6 and layer 5, just as layer 6 is part of layer 5 and layer 4, and so on. This is true all the way through to the core, or our physical body. Amazingly, this format replicates the layering in the afterlife as well, since the afterlife also consists of multiple, concentric layers within each other. This same format exists everywhere, including energies around all matter and every universal sphere. This is too consistent and structured to have come into existence from random force, so there must be some type of intelligent energy that created this refined organization. This gives rise to views about a higher power.

The Etheric Body

The first energy body we should consider is the etheric body, which is approximately one-quarter to two inches away from your physical body and is connected to the root, or first, chakra. This energy body resonates at nearly twenty cycles per minute, and through Kirlian photography is perceived to be in the bluish-gray color spectrum. The etheric body is an exact template of our physical body and holds the blueprints to our organs, muscles, tissues, and bones. The etheric body has no life of its own but interpenetrates the physical body. With the death of the physical body, the etheric body carries the other bodies away and later dissolves, and its energy is returned to the general etheric field. Once the etheric body has dissolved, the physical body begins to decompose. This energy body exists as matter in the lower etheric plane (in other words, part of our "spirit" is seen as matter in the afterlife), but soon gives way to the emotional, mental and astral bodies above it.

The Emotional Body

The next energetic body is the emotional body, which is the aura's second layer and interpenetrates the first layer. It can be seen about one inch to about four inches away from the body. This layer is connected to the sacral, or second, chakra and reflects a person's mood. Unlike the first layer, which totally contours the physical body, the emotional body's shape remains in constant motion. The color can be anything—depending on one's current mood and emotional well-being and is often associated with a rainbow of hues. Any disconnect or imbalance in this layer will heavily impact the first and third layers.

The Mental Body

Visible about three inches to eight inches away from the physical body is the mental body, or the third energy layer. You will see this layer, containing mostly your ideas, largely around the head and part of the shoulders and consisting of mostly yellow hues. This layer is connected to the solar plexus, or third, chakra of the body. This layer represents beliefs, power of understanding, intellect and thoughts and the way ideas, thoughts, and beliefs are validated and rationalized.

The Astral Body

Found about a foot away from the body, the astral body or fourth layer, is the link between the physical and spiritual bodies. This layer represents the bridge to the spiritual realm and is the doorway to the astral plane. This layer is connected with the heart chakra, which is likewise a bridge between the physical and the spiritual. The astral body enables us to leave our physical body while sleeping or in deep meditation, and temporarily visit the spiritual plane. While alive, we're still connected to our physical body via an elastic silver cord. This layer represents the ability to interact with people, love, and kinship. Once the astral body has separated from our lower energy bodies, our spiritual being, or soul, has left for the spiritual realm.

The Conceptual Body

The conceptual body is also known as the etheric template body, and it extends about one to two feet from the physical body. This is the spiritual copy of the physical body and is therefore unique to each person, just as the fingerprints are. Many describe this fifth layer as the carbon copy of the physical body, but in the spiritual plane. It connects with the throat (fifth) chakra, which represents creativity, vibration, communication, and sound.

The Celestial Body

The aura's sixth layer is the celestial body. Situated at a distance of about two to three feet from the body, this layer connects with the third eye (sixth) chakra. This layer represents the connectivity between the physical and spiritual mind, which is normally achieved through deep meditation. Often appearing as bright, shimmering opalescent colors, you become more aware of the celestial body as you raise your vibrations, level of awareness, and consciousness. As you work from the heart chakra to the sixth level, feelings of divine love and a connection with our fellow man become reality.

The Soul or Ketheric Body

This seventh layer, also known as the causal body, holds all other layers together and can extend out about three to five feet from the body. This layer appears gold in color and is shaped like an egg. This is the layer that is the "memory" of the immortal soul and contains all information and experiences the soul has undergone. It vibrates at the highest level and represents every experience physical and spiritual of the soul from inception until present. This is where the universe connects with the body; it is the link to the Divine and makes it possible to become one with It.

II

Can We Communicate With Spirit?

6

The Spirit Realms

"...the person who has passed into the spirit lands goes into his self-appointed place."
—Monsignor Robert Hugh Benson in "Here and Hereafter"

Most people wonder at some point in their life, "Where do we go when we die?" Others ask, "What is the transition like?" or "What do spirits do in the afterlife?" These seem to be age-old questions, yet on the surface there appears to be no satisfactory answer. Religious texts are typically the basis for most people's understanding of the afterlife. Christian texts historically point to a heaven with angels and harps for those who lived a "good" life based on the opinion of some type of all-knowing supreme being that hands down judgment upon those waiting to enter. For those unlucky enough to not make the cut, they are allegedly doomed to some type of hell for all eternity without the possibility of parole. If you didn't make heaven's first string, then you're sent to a purgatory until you're good enough.

This explanation never satisfied me, especially since I was

never raised with a strong religious influence. When I began thinking the church had been using fear of a hell and desire for a heaven as a way to control its followers for centuries, I really became skeptical. I felt mocked by any church official who said anything along the lines of, "Say ten Hail Marys and I can absolve you of your sins, my son." Who determined what a sin is anyway? Worse yet, the church appeared hypocritical and corrupt, especially in the Middle Ages, when it sold forgiveness through indulgences or implied that a person stood a better chance of getting into heaven with a larger donation.

To me it just sounded like a "pay to play" scheme. Because none of those explanations for the afterlife appeared genuine in my view, I largely turned away from religion. However, the barren wastelands of an agnostic viewpoint left me no comfort either, so I kept looking. I went searching for a better description from more neutral parties as well as those who seemed to have more firsthand knowledge. This included people who had well-documented NDEs as well as all the written accounts that existed in automatic writings over the last 150 years. The accounts one reads between NDEs and the spirit authors, over the last 150 years of automatic writings, is consistent and offers us great inspiration and hope. It appears that spirit authors are trying to inform us of certain spiritual "Truths" and help us raise our conscious and spiritual awareness.

To the casual reader, much of the material from NDEs and automatic writings is rather fanciful and initially creates skepticism. However, there are hundreds of writings from countless authors whose information is perfectly consistent over the last century and a half. As Victor Zammit, a well-known trial attorney, once opined, the sheer volume and consistency of evidence presented in support of the spirit world, as well as the credibility of the numerous witnesses, would be enough for a jury to find in favor of its existence.[4] The reading list I've included contains a section dedicated to automatic writings as well as NDEs on which much of the material below is based. That list just touches the tip of the proverbial iceberg of all the well-documented NDEs and automatic writings that exist worldwide.

Transition

Perhaps one of the most common questions clients ask is, "What's death like?" Another I hear often is, "Is death painful?" According to the many spirit authors, each transition is unique to the individual based on their expectations, mental state, and spiritual awareness at the time of passing. However, the overarching theme of love and compassion that embraces the new arrival remains the same for all.

Accounts describe the process of leaving our physical bodies as completely painless along with feelings of floating effortlessly, as there is no body about which to be concerned. Consider for a moment our etheric body and our consciousness, the energetic parts of us that travel beyond the physical body. Since we no longer need our physical body, we leave behind our material aspect of self and ego. All that remains is our energy, and we spirit beings take up residence in the nonphysical realm. For most of us, it is here that our spiritual journey truly begins, as we are no longer weighed down by earthly concerns. While we keep our personalities and individual characteristics, we become more centered on improving ourselves and try to learn the lessons we failed to learn while in the physical.

We all have a highly stretchable magnetic silver cord that connects our astral body to our physical body. The spirit body often withdraws from the physical body during sleep, while still connected by the silver cord. Think of it like an astronaut out on a spacewalk connected to his spaceship by a safety tether. This is why many people often have dreams that they've traveled to a far-off place or visited with people in different spheres—even our loved ones in spirit or our spirit guides. That's because we have.

However, at our point of transition to the spirit world, the silver cord disintegrates. Without anything holding down our etheric and astral bodies, they separate from our physical bodies—that is, we experience physical death. We feel nothing, it's just like astral traveling or dreaming. We see ourselves lifting from our physical shells, much like what NDE authors write as they see their bodies lying below them. Some spirits describe floating above their body, looking down on their old corpse, and perceiving it to be like a used dishrag with no purpose. Since this is just the etheric and astral bodies separating from the physical body, this is sometimes referred to as the "first" death.

The spirit person feels lighter, freer, and in better condition than they ever did in the physical. The aches and pains experienced while in the physical disappear, and physical limitations no longer exist. The paralyzed find they can jump and skip with joy. The blind can see perfectly. This is why so many spirits describe physical death as a great release. They no longer feel anything holding them back or feel any pain, but instead they live in their prime.

When they first pass into the spirit realm after physical death, the newly passed spirit is often confused and uncertain about where they are and what just happened. Many think they are dreaming, and some are unaware they have died. To help allay this predicament, there exists a group of loving souls whose primary job is to give a warm welcome to new arrivals, ease their entry, and alleviate their confusion. Part of the acclimation process includes the new spirit meeting with friends and relatives who are eager to show it a grand homecoming. As Monsignor Robert Hugh Benson said in *Here and Hereafter*, "In many cases, the gladness and happiness of these spirit friends cause the [new] spirit to believe that it is in heaven, or at least in a place of great happiness."[5]

For many, and based on their perception of earth before they passed, their new world appears virtually the same as it did when they were alive here in the physical. This is in part due to the power of thought, one of the most powerful forces in existence. Since the newly released spirit is now pure consciousness, it has unlimited abilities to use its thought powers to create its own existence. The power of the mind is unlimited. As John Milton wrote in *Paradise Lost*, "The mind is its own place, and in itself can make a heaven of hell, a hell of heaven."[6]

The new spirit transitions to a plane that exists at the same vibrational frequency its spirit bodies resonated at while on earth due to the Law of Attraction. This allows the person to arrive in the afterlife with a smooth, almost imperceptible transition that is more akin to an evolution than a revolution. Whatever mental, emotional, and spiritual state a person had accumulated over the long term while on earth, their energy body carries a corresponding energetic vibration. The energy plane on which the person arrives after physical death is determined by the specific frequency at which the energy body vibrates at the time of death.

Some spirits are initially confused because based on their religious upbringing and customs, they have preconceived notions about what heaven should look like or what the death process should be. Unfortunately, many of these beliefs and customs don't match the reality of the afterlife, which sometimes causes new spirits to either believe they haven't passed or causes them to wait for a dogmatic view of heaven that won't arrive.

Luckily, this is why beloved family or friends in spirit come to meet the soul that has recently crossed over, explain to the individual that they have died, and urge them to progress to the light. When the newly deceased clearly sees and speaks with their previously deceased family members or friends, that is usually enough to convince them they too have passed on to the nonphysical. In cases such as these, they move comfortably into the light and continue their spiritual progression.

However, sometimes a person may have such strong expectations of what heaven should look like or may have such a diminished degree of conscious awareness that their new reality causes utter confusion and they enter a lost state. In this case, the new spirit may get stuck between the physical and nonphysical planes. These entities are referred to as "earth-bound" spirits—ghosts. Usually they can be helped to the light by loving people in the physical who explain their predicament. This occurs because an earth-bound spirit is energetically closer to the physical and thus pays more attention to those in the physical. Spirit Rescue accomplishes this when a medium communicates with the spirit and attempts to raise the spirit's conscious awareness to include other versions of reality.

Once, for example, a stockbroker died in his office from a heart attack but couldn't be convinced by his previously deceased friends who met him that he had passed on. His focus remained on material things, especially money. He had no belief in anything outside of the physical, which kept him closer to the material plane. Finding their efforts to no avail, his friends in spirit left the man to find out about his condition on his own. He remained convinced he was still alive, for he appeared to still have a body (astral and etheric) and was able to speak to his coworkers in the physical as normal. When they didn't respond to him, he yelled as loud as he could, but they couldn't hear him. Even his body lying on the floor of his office didn't convince him.

He discovered he could hear everyone's conversations, including those far away about pending deals that affected his stocks. Curious about this newfound ability, he decided to whisper the new information to his friends in the office and see what would happen. To his surprise, his friends seemed to act on his information, and they began to profit. The man found this so enjoyable that he continued this for many years, even as his old friends died off and younger men took their place. Hence, his spirit lingered in the office. This is just one example where a person refused to acknowledge his new status among the deceased, causing him to exist as a nonphysical entity on the physical plane.

After spirit people become acclimated to their new environment, they experience what's often referred to as the *life review*. Some say it's similar to an instant movie of their entire life. This displays every action the individual conducted, both positive and negative, from the perspective of the *recipient*.

The new spirit viscerally understands how its actions affected others, from the intended recipient to all the adjacent people who were affected by that same action, including family and friends.

One example that has always stuck out for me was the life review experienced by a hit man who beat up and killed people for the mob without remorse. The review repeatedly put him in the shoes of those people whose lives he affected. He got to experience everything he had ever done to everyone in his past from the perspective of his victims, from appalling abuse to agonizing torture and death. He also felt the pain and suffering of his victims' relatives. After feeling firsthand this bombardment of agony, anguish, and grief that he had caused, the man screamed at the top of his voice, fell to his knees, and begged for the review to stop. He clearly learned his lesson.

Most life reviews, of course, are not quite so dramatic, but they are always instructive. Spirits are able to look back on their physical lives and perceive how they might have lived a better life or understand what different actions could have been taken. This is borne out during mediumship readings. Often loved ones in spirit return in a reading to apologize for hurtful actions, ask for forgiveness, or express regret, things that, given their ego, they might not have asked for while on earth. It's clear that death is not a "get out of jail free" occurrence. If a person has unresolved problems when they pass on, they carry those issues with them into spirit. However, those issues are dealt with from a perspective of love and compassion.

How the Spirit World Is Organized

Many spirits have written that the spirit world has seven concentric spheres, each with multiple levels. The best analogy for this is Russian nesting dolls, which are a set of wooden dolls of increasing size placed one over another. The smallest doll is by definition part of each successively larger doll. While the larger doll encompasses the smaller one, the smaller doll can't expand into or beyond the larger doll. Another analogy is the different layers of the ocean. The top layer is the brightest and warmest because it is closest to the source of light; the layer below it is slightly less bright, and the one below that even less so. There is no specific demarcation line between each layer, and each layer is part of the whole. Furthermore, different species live in each layer based on comfort and their acclimation to that specific layer.

Spirit refers to the different planes as spheres because they encompass the earth, which is a sphere itself. Think of the earth as the smallest Russian nesting doll inside several others of increasing size. Similar to the energy bodies, each successive sphere vibrates at a higher frequency and contains greater degrees of knowledge and love. Spirits who do not vibrate at a frequency corresponding to the next higher level can't travel to the next plane without accompaniment of one who has already achieved that higher level. It's not that they are not allowed, but the energy and light is so brilliant that the spirit finds existence at that higher level to be extremely uncomfortable and doesn't want to go there. Conversely, spirits can always move to lower planes without any problems because they have higher vibrations than the lower spheres do. It's all about where the spirit finds a natural level of comfort given their own vibration rate, similar to the Law of Attraction. The underlying concept behind the Law of Attraction stems from Buddha, who said, "All that we are is a result of what we have thought."[7]

The accounts from many NDEs describe a long, dark tunnel leading to an intense, bright light. Once in the light, the individual commonly sees a loved one they recognize who telepathically tells them how much they're loved, and also shares various aspects about the individual's life. A common ending to NDEs is the spirit telling the person that it's not their time yet to join the spirit realms, and they must return to the physical. This typically upsets the individual as they find this new existence so much more ideal and beautiful than earth that they want to stay and have no desire to return. Occasionally, the greeter will give the individual the choice to stay in spirit or return to their family on earth, which creates an entirely new dilemma for the person near a transition. Only a few individuals, self-described "selfish materialists," have depicted an NDE that sounded like a version of hell. However, this seems more linked to the person's preconceived religious perception, since their view of hell looked like Dante's *Inferno*.

Interestingly, automatic writings never describe this "tunnel of light" that most NDEs detail. One theory put forth is that this black tunnel leading to a bright light represents a method to insulate or block any view of the first- or lowest-vibration sphere, which could potentially traumatize a person with higher vibration rates if they saw it. Instead of seeing the first sphere, a transitioning individual or person having an NDE would only see bright spheres. Conversely, some individuals who have experienced NDEs—the "selfish materialists"—who felt they directly entered the lowest sphere, without any protection of the tunnel at all.

According to spirit authors in their automatic writings, levels are in effect stacked one above the other similar to concentric rings above the earth. However, the confusion seems to enter due to human translation of the concept. We think in terms of distance, while spirit is thinking in terms of its awareness of our plane due to its vibration rates. The higher a spirit's vibration stemming from its spiritual growth and evolution, the less focused its awareness on the earth plane as the gap between high and low vibration rates widens. This is similar to our low awareness of the spirit world. Yet since it is easier for spirit to travel to lower vibration spheres, it has a greater ability to visit us whenever they desire.

First, Second, and Third Spheres

The first sphere is typically considered a realm for less developed spirits who carry quite low vibrations and lack of love in their aura. Due to the lack of love, which is the source of light, there is little to no light in this lowest-vibration sphere, so typically it is dark. It's important to understand that the squalid conditions that exist in this region are *self-created* due to one's own perception of reality, as most spirits on this plane believe they don't deserve love. This is commonly referred to as the Shadowlands by spirits who have described it in automatic writing. Once the spirit learns to forgive itself and perceive love (which may take a very long time), it is then in a position to be rescued by highly evolved spirits who take on the very special job of rescuing souls from their own torment and help them up to higher levels.

Eighteenth-century philosopher and mystic Emanuel Swedenborg described the first sphere when he came through in an automatic writing for lawyer James E. Padgett in 1915:

In the spirit world, hell is a place, as well as a condition; and as a place, it has all the accompaniments that make it a reality to the spirits who inhabit it. The condition of the spirits who are in these hells is determined by their recollections worked upon by their consciences. There are, of course, no fires or brimstone lakes or devils with pitchforks adding to the sufferings of these spirits, but yet, there are certain conditions and appearances that are outside of the spirits themselves that cause their recollection to become more acute and to work in a manner to produce a greater degree of suffering.[8]

The second sphere is considered the sphere of familiarity, for it is the most similar to the earth in nearly all respects. This is where most people initially transition to—those who were not particularly spiritually minded and just did the best they knew how. The homes, streets, and trees will seem familiar, and friends and family are easy to find here. This sphere has trees, grass, animals, houses, hills, mountains, rivers, oceans, and everything beautiful one could imagine on earth.

Helen Padgett (wife of James E. Padgett) wrote the following about the second sphere:

The new spirit is met by family and friends who have gone before, with love, kindness and consolation at a lovely greeting place, but eventually every soul must find its home according to its soul condition. Then comes a time when that soul must stand alone in its weakness or strength and realize that no other can bear its sorrows or take from its burdens or enter into its suffering. I can envision a spirit welcoming committee of family and friends lined up according to their closeness and love for the new spirit. I would also say that often the welcoming place is a nicer one than the home that the spirit has made for itself by how it lived on the earth.[9]

Spiritualist Arthur Findlay wrote of the second sphere:

A surprise for some who have made their transition will be to see the stately buildings, comfortable houses, gardens, cities, pets, all sorts of games, sports, amusements; and the pleasures of science, art, music and literature, and to be able to continue those things that were of interest in the earth life.[10]

The similarity of the second sphere to the earth is one of the reasons new spirits occasionally get confused and initially have trouble understanding that they have passed out of the physical.

The nonphysical life carries far more brilliant aspects for each sense, while the earth appears far more muted in every respect. For example, rather than seeing a sun in the sky at a fixed point, spirits have described bright light coming from every object and every direction, as if every object was a sun and emitted light. There are no clouds or rain or weather, so it's always bright. It is also warm and comfortable. In fact, most spirits describe this and subsequent spheres as Summerland, since it seems to be like a perpetual summer paradise. Because nothing decays, since everything is pure energy in the spirit world, everything lives eternally. This implies no dirt or dust or disintegration of any item.

The second and third levels have colors similar to those on earth, except there are so many more hues that humans never have experienced on earth; the diversity of color makes a dazzling array to the eyes. Furthermore, the colors aren't just more vivid and in a broader spectrum, but they create beautiful music and gorgeous sounds, the likes of which humans have never heard, based on the specific hue. Combined, the colors and sounds form a living, breathing existence throughout nature that comes alive.

Additionally, water shines and sends forth brilliant colors, which themselves sing special tunes based on the colors. The water is always the perfect temperature and always enables people to float, swim, or boat wherever and whenever they want. Everything is alive with light, color, and music, giving rise to the saying that spirits feel more alive in the spirit world than they ever did when they were alive on earth.

Spirit constructs buildings and homes for the sheer enjoyment of it, not because of any need for shelter or warmth. If they want a feeling of a vast space with beauty and decorations, they might prefer to create and live in a mansion. Others are more comfortable living in a small house similar to one they grew up in. They might want to exactly replicate their childhood bedroom. Should they want to change any of these, then they imagine something new. Whatever the mind wants, the mind creates, for the power of thought is pervasive in the spirit world.

The third sphere is the first sphere where the spirit resides as a result of a devotional path of progress, either as a result of a life on earth or since coming to the spirit realms. Starting with the third sphere, the vibration rates substantially increase, while the focus or concern for material or earthly matters begins to dissipate. The higher up the levels a spirit progresses, the greater the quality of spirituality and love it gains.

Helen Padgett described her home on the third sphere after

progressing from the second sphere like this:

Yes, my [new] home is very beautiful and I am perfectly delighted with it. It is made of white marble and is surrounded by lawns and flowers and trees of various kinds. The grass is so very green and the flowers are so beautiful and variegated. The trees are always in foliage and have such beautiful limbs and leaves. I am most pleased with my home—I mean the building. There are many beautiful pictures on the walls, and the walls are all frescoed and hung with fine coverings. And the floors are inlaid with beautiful mosaics. I have all the splendid furniture that I could possibly wish for, and my library is full of books of all kinds—especially those that tell of God and His Love for man. You would be in your element if you could be with me.

I have music such as you never heard on earth, and instruments of various kinds which I am learning to play. And I sing with all my heart and soul as the days go by. I have beds on which I lie down, but I never sleep. We do not need sleep here; we only rest. For sometimes we get tired from our work, and are greatly refreshed by lying on the beds and couches which are so comfortable that we do not realize that we are tired after lying down a little while.

We eat fruit and nuts not because we are hungry, but more because we enjoy the flavors. They are like pears, grapes, oranges and pomegranates—of course not just the same, as you know them. We do not actually eat these things with our teeth and palate or use our intestinal organs, as you do, but we imbibe, as it were, the delicious flavors and aromas of the fruits; and, strange as it may seem, we are just as satisfied, and probably more so than when you eat these things with your physical organs.[11]

A Spirit's Path

A spirit has three possible paths of progress up to higher levels in the spirit world. The first path is the Development of the Intellect. Spirit can progress along this path by increasing its powers of thought and reason, such as by studying science and medicine. Spirits progressing on this path typically reside on spheres two, four, and six. The second path is the Purification of Human Love. While all humans have this natural love in their souls, it must be purified by expressing good thoughts and deeds, otherwise known as the Golden Rule. While spirits progressing on this path also use spheres two, four, and six, they use different levels or planes on those spheres. The final path is the most spiritual, as it develops a relationship with God by acquiring God's divine love. Spirits use spheres three, five, and seven for this path as they progress. Few spirits have completed their spiritual progress beyond the seventh sphere, which is the most focused on God.

Directly above the seventh sphere in energetic vibrations is the Spiritual Kingdom, also known as heaven. According to some spirit authors, this realm is not as old as the lower planes, as it was created at the time of Jesus's birth. The kingdom carries a great deal of spiritual importance because its purpose is the redemption of all humanity.

A. G. Riddle (law partner of James E. Padgett) wrote of the Spiritual Kingdom in an automatic writing:

The Kingdom, as a place, is real and independent of the state of the soul, though it is necessary for the soul to be in a corresponding state in order to enter the kingdom. The many mansions spoken of [in the Bible] are there and change not, and whether they shall have occupants depends upon the soul's harmony with the laws of God to enter this kingdom.[12]

The most important takeaway from spirits' descriptions is that in the spirit world, they create with their thoughts. This sounds like many of the great philosophers who have said that "Thoughts become things," or, in Buddha's words, "All that we are is a result of what we have thought." We in the physical should learn from spirit and should apply this truism, for it has been shown countless times that our thoughts influence our reality.

What Spirits Do In the Afterlife

On more than one occasion, spirit has clearly emphasized that it is very active in the afterlife and trying to grow spiritually. The spirit of a young man told his mother in a reading I gave, "I'm not up here just playing harps and eating bonbons, ya know." This shows that spirit people keep their personalities and are quite active. What we do in the afterlife typically depends on the sphere on which we arrived, and later, the path of progress we choose to take. Nevertheless, it's clear that regardless of the sphere or the path, spirit seeks to improve the amount of love and kindness it gives others, for love is the fabric of the spirit world.

Spirit's love is an unconditional and selfless love of humanity and caring for the well-being of others. Once a spirit gets acclimated to its surroundings, it finds that quite often the activities it prefers are those that help others improve themselves, just as it had been helped by more evolved souls. Often, spirits will take a position in which they can return the favor given to them when they arrived.

For example, if a spirit received help in its transition from special greeters, then it may in turn learn how to be a greeter to other newly arrived souls. Some spirits prefer tending to new arrivals in spirit rest homes. These new arrivals may have had a traumatic passing or a difficult time adjusting to the spirit world. Much the same way earth has hospitals with practitioners helping us heal, the spirit world has rest facilities with loving souls who help bring the individual back to spiritual health. Though many confuse these workers with angels, they're just loving spirit people who want to help their fellows. These are also ways for these spirits to progress.

Most spirits seem focused on learning and expanding their knowledge in specific areas, for the spirit world is a world of both love and learning, if not a love of learning. Some spirits choose to learn more about helping others, some seek a closer understanding of God, some choose to expand their understanding of science, and others continue their work with music. Spirits tend to continue with activities they truly loved while in the physical. The choices, as you can imagine, are endless. Often scientists, doctors, artists, musicians, and authors in spirit create new works and love to share them with others both in spirit and in the physical.

For example, when Mozart composed his Symphony no. 1 in E flat major, he wrote it at the tender age of eight! How was he able to do this? Clearly this was no ordinary activity. Spirit has said they gave Mozart much of his musical inspiration. Similarly, Nicolas Tesla was a genius of electrical and mechanical machinations, as da Vinci was with early inventions. Others include Archimedes (in ancient Greece),

Franklin, Edison, and Westinghouse, just to name a few. The same can be said for famous artists, including Michelangelo, da Vinci, Raphael, Van Gogh, Moreau, Picasso, Matisse, Monet—and the list goes on. The one thing all of these great thinkers, inventors, artists and musicians had in common was incredible inspiration.

However, the spirit world isn't all work; providing inspiration for others is only one small piece. Joy is a central theme in the afterlife, often fulfilled by music, theater, and praise to God for His love. Great, classical musical works are performed with huge choirs, often directed by the original composers themselves. Likewise, elaborate and historic plays are staged (many of which are comedies), again with the original playwright either acting in or directing the performance. When attention gets turned to the Divine, beautiful music and gorgeous colors emanate from the hall where the concert or service is being conducted.

What the Afterlife Feels Like

Quite often spirits make it abundantly clear that they feel more alive in the spirit world than they did in the physical. They say they feel like they were previously sleeping and that earth life felt like a bad dream from which they've finally awoken. Spirit people indicate they have dramatically heightened sensitivity and greatly enhanced awareness.

One account offers this analogy: It's as if previously a person was in a dark and silent warehouse, and he was only aware of things he could see in front of him, illuminated within a narrow beam of light from a flashlight. Nothing else in the warehouse could be seen, heard, or known. Suddenly the lights in the warehouse get turned on; everything can be seen from a 360-degree perspective, and dramatic colors never before experienced are presented in a kaleidoscopic effect, with beautiful music as a harmonious backdrop. This dichotomy of awareness between two worlds is how people in spirit have often portrayed the differences between the physical and the nonphysical.

Other reports from NDEs and automatic writings from spirit authors suggest just how enhanced their sensitivity and awareness have become. They describe a world that feels like an endless tapestry whose fabric is made of love. They suggest that everyone's individual essence is like a thread in a giant tapestry that interconnects with the essence of everyone we have ever known. Every action we take in our lives affects everybody else throughout existence at all times without our knowledge.

This is supported by quantum physics' theory of entanglement, in which a group of particles interact in a such way that the quantum state of each particle of the group cannot be described or measured independently of the state of the others, regardless of the distance. In a 1935 paper, Albert Einstein referred to this as "spooky action at a distance." Entanglement theory is similar to the "Butterfly Effect," often associated with the work of Edward Lorenz, in which a small change in one place has broad impacts in far distant places.[13]

Consequently, we are all connected to one another and are part of All That Is, creating a unity of existence.

7

The Differences Between Spirit Guides and Angels

"Your Spirit Guides and Angels will never let you down as you build a rapport with them. In the end, they may be the only ones who don't let you down."
— Linda Deir

Whether or not you believe in them or have yet to make contact, you have at least one guide who is present to assist you, provided you keep it in your thoughts. The primary disagreement about spirit guides revolves around whether they are permanently with you from birth or if they need to be invited into your life. From what I've come to learn, it's a combination of the two options, though I'm sure I'll find out for sure once I join the spirit world. While your main guide is initially present with you from birth, unless you invite it to participate in your life as you mature, that guide may eventually move on to help others. The moment you ask for your guide's assistance, it will gladly offer help. Thus a guide's help depends on you.

What Is a Spirit Guide?

A spirit guide is a soul that has reached an elevated point in its evolution; it is aware and expanded enough to assist another soul in their spiritual growth. Guides have previously incarnated as humans, so they understand the difficulties of the human experience. They are capable of a level of nonjudgment, compassion, and love that most of us can only imagine. They are highly trained in their missions.

Spirit guides have consciously and purposely taken on the role of being a guide. They want to assist you; it's their job. Your guides are deeply invested in you because the expansion of their own spiritual awareness comes from serving the human world. They can't intervene in your life unless you ask. I encourage you to find a way to cultivate an awareness of and a relationship with your guides. When you created your plan to reincarnate to this world, you had several guides agree to come with you specifically to help you keep on track with your life purpose.

Guides are like friends but with greater wisdom and unconditional love available. Depending on your needs, you may have more than one guide at any one time, though you usually have one primary guide who is considered the organizer and leader. This main guide is often referred to as a Master Guide. You receive guides at different ages and stages of life depending on your needs. You have an inner band of seven spirit guides that are available to you most of your life, and an outer band consisting of specialist guides you can call on when needed. These specialty guides are similar to specialty contractors that come in for specific jobs.

Spirit guides usually fulfill different roles in your life.

Master Guides

Your Master Guide is the manager or director of your spirit team. This is the guide you will see most frequently. Its role is to direct the rest of your spirit team and act as your go-to person. It heads up your team and has been involved in many of your incarnations. Your Master Guide is usually a member of your soul family. The Master Guide teaches you soul lessons and inspires you to fulfill your destiny and is often your Teacher Guide.

Gatekeeper Guides

Your Gatekeeper Guide is the bouncer of your spirit team. Its role is to keep you safe. This guide offers physical and psychic protection to all spirit communicators, allowing only higher vibrational energies and the most appropriate spirits to work with you. The Gatekeeper also ensures that spirits don't crowd you and only approach you one at a time.

The Gatekeeper is strong in manner and character and often has a large, strong etheric body to match. It is often of indigenous heritage to wherever you live or of your ancestry. While often human in appearance, it can also appear as a larger animal such as an elephant, panther, or wolf. You call on the Gatekeeper when you need strength, courage, and bravery … or to have with you all the time as a spiritual protector to watch over you.

Message Bearer (Messenger) Guides

The Message Bearer Guide assists you in finding and obtaining information; improving your ability to get, hear, and deliver messages from the spirit world; and in developing clairaudient or clairvoyant skills. Many psychics, mediums, and those who work in the Akashic Records use Message Bearer Guides during readings and for the information they provide to others. While Message Bearer Guides are usually humans, they can appear in the form of a bird, usually a hawk or eagle, because of their ability to travel great distances in a short amount of time to obtain information quickly and swiftly with little detection, which can be quite helpful.

Healing Guides

Your Healing Guide helps you with your spiritual, emotional, and physical health. This is the medic of your spirit team. This guide is responsible for healing your energy field and chakras, as well as teaching you how to heal yourself and others. They are excellent guides for anyone working in a healing profession such as energy healing or surgery. However, you may connect with a Healing Guide to improve your well-being. These guides were often healers in their time on earth, and often appear as ancient monks, Old-World shamans, and spiritual healers on the other side.

Teacher Guides

Your Teacher Guide helps you with your spiritual growth. The Teacher Guide assists with your soul's growth, teaching you things related to the life lessons you are here to learn. It directs you to books you need to read and classes you need to take, and it introduces you to new and necessary physical teachers here on earth. Teacher Guides assist you in understanding the philosophical and spiritual aspects of any studies you undertake while on earth. Teacher Guides help you learn your lessons through action.

Joy Guides

Typically your Joy Guide is an uplifting source of energy that tries to boost your spirits when you're feeling glum or just sort of ho-hum. It helps you enjoy your physical life and bring opportunities in your path that help bring feelings of happiness and love.

Joy Guides more often than not appear to you as a young child (often a little girl), symbolizing youthful energy, innocence, happiness, joy (obviously), fun, and bubbly effervescence. Imagine all the traits of a happy young child, and that is your Joy Guide wrapped into a package. Think of Tinker Bell, Peter Pan, or any other young, happy fantasy character, and you begin to understand what a Joy Guide can do. I find one of the most important guides in everyone's life is probably a Joy Guide.

My Joy Guide

For the longest time I was aware there were Joy Guides and that everyone had one, but I grew frustrated that I hadn't met mine yet. I knew I was often surrounded by spirit guides because I often felt warm, tingly sensations. These are the classic signs of spirit guides. My problem was I didn't know which guide was causing the tingling sensations, so one day two years after my awakening, I finally decided to figure it out.

As I sat at my desk thinking about my different guides, it slowly dawned on me that every time I had these tingling sensations, they were in the exact same place—on my upper arms/shoulder joints. It was like spirit's calling card. My difficulty lay in my inability to differentiate the subtle differences between the sensations. So I thought back to the *feelings* associated with the physical perceptions. I realized that on certain occasions when I experienced sensations that were slightly more bubbly than normal, a big smile crossed my face. I figured those *had* to have been from my Joy Guide, since I smiled and felt quite happy each time I had that particular sensation. When I realized that, a miraculous thing happened ... I heard and saw my Joy Guide—finally!

I suddenly heard clairaudiently a little girl start to shout "Yaaaaay!" Simultaneously I clairvoyantly saw her do a back flip, and balloons quickly floated up into the air like a party had started. The little girl had curly, blonde hair down to her shoulders with rays of sun shining through it, and a giant daisy rested on her right ear. She looked like she was shouting for joy, and her arms were outstretched with both of her thumbs pointing up to the sky. Her little face was absolutely adorable with perfectly clean, white skin.

When I asked what her name was, I also heard clairvoyantly (before I'd even finished the question) the name "Priscilla" spoken in a little girl's voice. Definitely not a name I was expecting (or even hear anymore), so I have no doubt it wasn't my imagination. Heck, it didn't even sound like my own voice. After I heard Priscilla's voice, I Googled the word *joy* and searched for an image associated with the word. I froze when I saw the picture on my computer screen. It looked uncannily like the girl I'd seen in my mind's eye. I admit this sounds pretty farfetched, and it's still difficult for me to comprehend. But that's the way spirit works.

Now whenever I need a little sunshine in my life or a little pick-me-up, I just call on Priscilla, and my whole outlook on the world feels like a warm, sunny day in summer. It puts a big smile on my face. Imagine the happy little girl I described above appearing in your life—how could you not be happy? I think it's important for *everyone* to meet their own Joy Guide so they can experience greater happiness in their life.

My Gatekeeper and Teacher Guides

Though I often feel a typical calling card or sign from my spirit guides, occasionally I won't. Instead, I'll receive a magnificent clairvoyant image of them, letting me know they're nearby. During one meditation, I encountered both my protector and teacher guides as totem animals.

In my mind's eye grew a scene displaying the shore of a large lake in the early morning's first light. Tall green pine trees surrounded the water's edge, and majestic, snow-covered mountains stood in the distance. It was cold outside, and steam was rising off the flat, still surface of the water. The still water acted as a giant mirror reflecting the trees, mountains, and cloudless blue sky. It was difficult to tell where the water ended and the land began. I sat by an extinguished campfire in front of an old tent near the rocky shore. From head to toe, I wore the furry skins of animals I'd hunted. The fur and fat kept me extremely warm, and the oil on the fur kept the skins quite water resistant.

Movement in the woods off to my left caused me to look that direction. Soon a beautiful lone wolf come out of the forest, on to the left shoreline, and approached me. It was strong and lean, with a soft pelt of shiny, gray fur. The wolf didn't appear menacing or threatening. I sensed it was friendly and that we had known each other a long time. Somehow I knew it had been previously working in the background protecting and shepherding me.

Now, however, the wolf felt comfortable drawing close to me and standing by my side. I felt tremendous respect and love between us, almost like old friends feel. It soon lay down on my left side and looked back to where it had entered the clearing. A brilliant white light surrounded the wolf, suggesting to me that it was a spirit guide.

I then got a sense of a large bird flying high above me to my right, like a hawk, falcon, or eagle. When I looked up, I saw the bird had a large, yellow, hooked beak, a wide wingspan, and a white head, suggesting to me it might be a bald eagle. The eagle flew closer and eventually landed on my right shoulder. Despite its large size and sharp talons, I never felt it actually touch my shoulder, which made me think this too might be a spirit guide. I gathered it must be a forward lookout for the wolf and could see miles in any direction. This gave me the impression that the eagle was my Teacher Guide, who had much information to pass on to me.

What Is an Angel?

Like spirit guides, angels are also available for guidance and protection, and they embody unconditional love, compassion, and wisdom. Some people say they have an angel as one of their spirit guides—which, given their characteristics, is entirely reasonable. Most spiritual traditions describe angels as messengers of God, full of His love and carrying His love to humans on earth. However, angels have never incarnated in human form, which separates them from spirit guides who have previously incarnated. There seems to be agreement among different heritages that there is a hierarchy of angels, organized by function.

We may talk to angels and pray to them—although typically they aren't to be worshipped. Some belief systems suggest we all have a guardian angel whose primary job is to watch over us and protect us. You can probably think of some close calls you've had in your life when you were delivered from harm. Guardian angels keep us safe in situations like these and work through our intuition to guide us away from dangerous choices. Angels are interwoven in the culture of humans. Regardless of religion or belief system, stories of angels are a part of humans' heritage and a piece of the fabric that makes up human history. References to angels often refer specifically to an archangel.

Archangels

Archangels are probably the most well-known outside of a strictly religious context. They are considered to be very powerful spiritual beings who have captured our attention for centuries. The prefix *arch* means *ruling* or *chief* in Greek.[14] Religious texts refer to an archangel as being at a high level in the celestial hierarchy. Many scriptures tell of the archangels' great abilities as healers and guides that intervene with assistance in many of life's challenging situations. Most traditions and faiths reference seven archangels, and they govern different areas of life.

Michael

Archangel Michael is the angel most called upon for protection and guidance. His name means *He who is as God,* and he is most often thought of as the angel of protection and the most powerful of all the angels. Michael is an exceptionally strong angel who protects and defends people who love God. He is powerfully concerned about truth, justice, and integrity. He is considered a leader within the angelic realm and a patron angel of righteousness, mercy, and justice. As such, scriptural artwork depicts him as a warrior, most often carrying a sword. Archangel Michael assists in situations where you are afraid, confused, or concerned for your safety. He helps support you in making life changes and is often said to work closely with people who perform healing work or provide spiritual teaching. Other areas where Archangel Michael can be of assistance include courage, direction, energy, and vitality, all aspects of life purpose, motivation, space clearing, worthiness, and self-esteem.

Raphael

Archangel Raphael, whose name means *God heals*, is the archangel designated for physical and emotional healing. Archangel Raphael not only helps in healing individuals, but also helps healers in their healing practice. He can help reduce addictions and cravings and is powerful in healing other injuries and illnesses, with cures often occurring immediately. Archangel Raphael aids in restoring and maintaining harmony and peace. He is also the patron of travelers, watching over them to ensure a safe and harmonious journey. Working in conjunction with Archangel Michael, Archangel Raphael helps to clear away fears and stressors that may be adversely affecting your health.

Gabriel

Archangel Gabriel's name means *God is my strength*. One of the two archangels specifically named in both the Old and New Testaments of the Bible, she is often portrayed holding a trumpet. As the patron of communications, Archangel Gabriel is a messenger angel, acting as a messenger of God. She helps writers, teachers, journalists, and artists to convey their message, to find motivation and confidence, and to market their skills. She also assists in overcoming issues of fear and procrastination in communication as well as in all areas related to children, helping during conception, pregnancy, childbirth, and child-rearing.

Jophiel

The patron saint of artists, Archangel Jophiel's name means *Beauty of God.* She helps us see and maintain beauty in life and supports us in thinking beautiful thoughts and in staying positive; she also offers support in creating and manifesting beauty in our surroundings and our hearts. Archangel Jophiel assists us in slowing down and bringing calm to our lives, heals negativity and chaos, helps to tame egos, and bring organization to a place or situation. When seeking wisdom or a shift in perspective, Archangel Jophiel is the archangel to call in to uplift you and help you see things from a different point of view.

Ariel

The patron angel of animals and the environment, Archangel Ariel's name means *lion or lioness of God.* Her role is to protect the earth, its natural resources, ecosystems, and wild life, and she is always available with support and guidance for any activities that involve protecting, healing, rejuvenating, and/or maintaining our environment. Archangel Ariel assists in healing injured animals and works closely with Archangel Raphael in these endeavors. She assists in providing insights and opportunities to expand your awareness and experience. Ariel inspires people on earth to create great art and make great scientific discoveries, and encourages people to live up to God's full potential for them by discovering and fulfilling God's purposes for their lives. Since Archangel Ariel is watching over the earth's natural resources, she can also be especially helpful in ensuring your needs for food, water, shelter, and other supplies are met.

Azrael

Archangel Azrael's name means *Whom God helps.* However, he is often referred to as *The Angel of Death.* Azrael meets souls and helps them in the transition of death, in addition to helping newly crossed-over souls adjust. He also helps loved ones who are still on the earth plane in dealing with their grief and processing the loss. Archangel Azrael helps ministers and spiritual teachers from all belief systems and religions in their spiritual counseling. He assists grief counselors in shielding themselves from absorbing their clients' pain while guiding their words and actions as well. This archangel assists in all types of transitions and endings, not just those involving loss and death. He also helps with transitions related to relationships, careers, and addictions, and helps us navigate as smoothly as possible through life's changes.

Chamuel

Archangel Chamuel's name means *He who sees God.* This archangel has been called by many names throughout history and thus is sometimes confused with other angels. His mission is to bring peace to the world, and he protects the world from fear and negative energies. He is believed to have all-knowing vision and the ability to see the interconnectedness between all things. Archangel Chamuel assists in finding strength and courage to face adversity when it seems we have neither left. He can also help us find lost items and solutions to problems, and he can help us find important parts of our lives such as life purpose, a love relationship, a new job, and supportive friendships. Finally, Archangel Chamuel also helps to heal anxiety, bring peace, and repair relationships and misunderstandings.

My Encounters with Angels

Despite all of my prior encounters, to this day I'm still somewhat hesitant to admit the existence of angels. I'm not sure if that's because they seem too closely related to religion or if their existence is just too fantastic for me to fully believe. You'd think that with all of my dramatic meditations and wonderful, affirmed connections with spirit through my readings that I'd be totally on board with angelic beings. Nevertheless, the skeptic inside me struggles to remain relevant.

Some of my experiences truly challenged my beliefs and made me wonder if I was being too critical. During one meditation, for example, as usual I noticed my upper arms and the sides of my shoulders begin to get that warm, tingling sensation. I usually interpret this as my spirit guides' calling card. However, this time my experience began to move beyond my typical spirit guide interaction.

I started to see in my mind's eye a vision of a beautiful young woman with bright white skin. Interestingly, however, she had a light-pink glow just under her eyes. She wore a garland of yellow flowers, perhaps small daisies, on the top of her head, and long, curly light brown hair fell past her shoulders. I began to think this was the same angelic being who previously visited me. Although the image was only from the center of her chest up to her face, I could tell she was wearing a nice, simple white dress. Her mouth began to move as if she were speaking, but I couldn't hear any words she was saying.

The image of the woman started to slightly change. She grew taller and appeared to now be wearing what looked like a nurse's hat on the top of her head. She still wore a white dress, although her long, curly hair became more blonde than light brown. As I continued to look at her in an effort to get more detail, I was astonished to see wings on her back!

At the same time, I heard in my head the name Ariel, which sounded familiar but didn't have much meaning to me. Mind you, I didn't know one angel from another at the time. However, this finally made sense to me later when I learned that Ariel is an angel who heals, provides insights to expand our awareness, inspires us, and encourages us to fulfill God's potential for our lives. After I made this connection with how my life was unfolding, I was absolutely stunned. This was no coincidence.

I had another experience during a short meditation, somewhat similar to one of the meditations I described during my period of awakening. I'd been surrounding myself with Divine energy by envisioning myself enveloped with white light. I asked my spirit guides of love, truth, and compassion to enter my aura and grace me with their presence. I sought the protection of all loving energies from the spirit realms and those that came from God.

No sooner had I finished those thoughts than I felt an intense tingling and warmth in my upper arms and the sides of my shoulders, as well as in my knees. This new sensation caught my attention, as I realized it must be a different spirit guide or a deeper level of contact. I began to see a small, fuzzy white beam of light in the distance. As the light drew closer and revealed more details, to my surprise I saw a wing attached on one side. Then two wings appeared.

As I continued to stare at this object, it became clear to me that this was a white angel with wings, just floating in front of me. It was a little fuzzy, but unmistakable. I just sat there dumbfounded. What was I to make of such an extraordinary experience, and how could I tell anyone? Surely no one would believe me. I didn't even believe it myself. However, these occurrences had been happening too many times to just dismiss out of hand. I just had to accept the events and hold them in my memory.

Angels are a fascinating aspect of our history as a culture. Whether you are a believer or a skeptic, your archangel can assist you whenever you call on them. Angels are extensions of the Divine, assisting us and carrying our prayers and messages back to the Source. They understand your life mission and want to help you accomplish it. Many have found connecting with an archangel who specializes in the area of their life where they would like to see improvement has accelerated positive progress and changes.

8

We Need To Start Listening More

"The universe is full of noise. True wisdom is in knowing what to pay attention to."
— Debasish Mridha

We live in a fast-paced world that keeps getting faster every day. We are glued to our mobile phones in search of the latest text or tweet and feel compelled to immediately respond to them. There are stories of people falling into uncovered manholes because they were glued to the texts on their phones. The Post Office used to deliver "snail mail." Now, email has become the slow communication service. God forbid anyone even bothers to pick up a phone to speak with someone, let alone practice the long-lost art of something once known as letter writing. Teens can't even talk to each other across a table. They can only communicate by texting. This has become a disturbing trend, which may make me sound old-fashioned. I hear that all the time from my eighteen-year-old son, who constantly reminds me that I live in the last century (or often many centuries ago).

Even when we're in communication with someone else, most of us are in such a rush to get our point across or respond to the other person's statement that we aren't bothering to really listen to each other anymore. Perhaps this is a result of our instant-messaging era. My wife and I are just as guilty of this as anyone else, something we remind each other of frequently. This may be a symptom of our loss of communication skills in addition to our high-paced society. We're so fast-paced now that we don't even give ourselves time to hear what's happening in our bodies or our minds. Furthermore, an increasing number of people are becoming unhealthier as they become stressed out and burned out and suffer from hypertension.

Calm the Mind, Listen to the Silence

We really need to slow down, relax our minds and bodies, and listen to everything around us. The most effective way to do this is through the ancient art of meditation, which helps to explain part of the reason why meditation has become so popular in modern society. As I discussed in the first chapter, at the time when I was highly stressed from my career in finance, I had little sleep, I got no exercise, I ate poorly, and as a result I was beginning to become emotionally unglued and took it out on my family. In an effort to learn how to relax, I turned to meditation.

In the beginning, it was a struggle to sit in one place for more than five minutes. I had to learn to keep my mind calm without allowing thousands of thoughts to go flying through my brain. But as I learned a few simple techniques to focus on one thing at a time, my meditation practice slowly became more steady. There's a saying that it takes about ninety days of repeated actions for something to become a habit. This old adage nearly proved true, for in about four months, meditation became a learned practice and habit that kept improving. Most important, I noticed that not only was I becoming calmer, but I could maintain my focus longer, and I was able to hear and notice unique sounds more clearly. I could see greater details and more colors; I could hear more notes and instruments in music; I heard people's words more clearly rather than a jumble of sounds; and I felt like I was beginning to open up to my surroundings. Granted, I still had a long, long way to go, but the change in the first few months was quite noticeable.

As I learned to quiet my mind, I became more aware of certain images, impressions, and feelings in my mind that didn't entirely feel like my own. They were just small at first, but they felt out of context and out of place relative to my stream of consciousness. I immediately set these "unowned" feelings aside, assuming they were my imagination. However, the more I was able to quiet my mind and listen to my surroundings, the more distinctive the impressions became. This lasted for about a year as my meditation grew deeper and longer. I began to play with the feelings and ask them questions, like what their names were, as if they were really people who might respond to me. I never expected any answer.

You can figure out what happened next. I immediately got two names—one for a woman, the other for a man. Without any hesitation, the beings impressed upon me that they were my spirit guides. That's when the floodgates opened up, and I knew I was in contact with the spirit world. I began searching for a greater understanding of the spirit world and how to more clearly communicate with it. The main takeaway I had from my early research and reading was the importance of learning how to calm the mind and listen to the silence, both activities that I practice as often as possible today.

Both the excessive speed of our daily activities and the cacophony of sounds that bombard us in modern times easily distracts us. By contrast, the pace of life was much slower in the late nineteenth and early twentieth centuries. People tended to stay home more, and when they were out they walked calmly everywhere. They also went to bed earlier and got a better night's rest.

These days, we don't get enough sleep, we're always stressed out about something, we zip everywhere we can in cars, and we seem to avoid even a modicum of exercise (although this is improving). Rarely is anyone ever accused of sitting in a garden and enjoying the peace and quiet for too long. As a result, it's difficult for anyone to regularly sit quietly and focus in an effort to bring through spirit and display its physical manifestations.

Why do I mention this? This comes full circle to the beginning of this chapter, namely that we can't hear ourselves think because we are running around multitasking or playing with electronics rather than "stopping to smell the roses." In an effort to reconnect with our loved ones in spirit, we have to get our minds in the right place, a place conducive to mental mediumship.

Consider for a second how difficult it would be to communicate telepathically with a living human being who is standing in front of you when you're on your phone texting, let alone communicate telepathically with a loved one in spirit in another dimension and energy state. There's no way any of that would ever happen because of the numerous distractions. However, place your mind in a calm state, with zero distractions where you can focus and feel the energy from the telepathic communication, and you'd be that much closer to achieving success. This is what we need to do to better prepare our minds and hearts to communicate with spirit. The calmer we are, the more loving we are, and the more focused we are, the better we can open to and listen for our spirit loved ones.

How Spirit Tries to Make Itself Known to Us Everyday

Even if we aren't fully open to spirits' communication, they do try to contact us and let us know they are with us. In fact, some of the more common questions I receive revolve around detecting spirit. For example, "If spirit is around everyone, then how do I know it's really around *me*?" Another one is, "Doesn't spirit only reveal itself to those with special skills?" Yet another question is, "How do I know that what I'm hearing and seeing isn't just my imagination?" Those are fair questions, questions that I had trouble answering myself for a long time. However, I learned that while it's fairly easy to discover spirit's presence, several things need to happen to let them come through fully.

Be open to the existence of spirit.

First and foremost, we must be open to the very existence of spirit, otherwise we'll never be able to interact with them. Know that spirit eagerly wants to communicate with us in some way (whether mental or physical) to let us know they're still here. However, universal law stipulates spirit cannot interfere with our free will, so they're not going to be overly active with us. Instead, they'll be so understated and low key that they seem hidden to us.

Just think of when your gut instinct is telling you to bring that umbrella because you sense there might be a chance of rain ... but you usually ignore it, and you get soaked later (happens to me more times than I care to think of). Or perhaps you're driving down the highway and you get the feeling that for some reason you should move over to the next lane ... but you ignore it, and because the car in front of you suddenly stops, you slam into it. Are these instances just sheer chance, coincidence, and timing, or is there something more happening behind the scenes?

These are perfect examples of spirit softly nudging you and making itself and its information known, but only if you *want* to accept it. It's sort of like a very soft-spoken advisor in spirit giving you information to do with what you want. Mmm, "spirit" + "advisor" ... sounds like a spirit guide, doesn't it? Or maybe it's a loved one in spirit trying to impart some wisdom somehow. Either way, when spirit tries to get a message to us, it's always so subtle, in such hushed tones and hidden methods that we don't normally recognize it as such. Yet that's just how spirit works—so softly that we must proactively search for it to understand it and see it. But once we understand this, that's why I answer "yes" to the question "Can Anyone Contact Spirit?"

Be aware of your state of mind.

Second, our state of mind influences our ability to be receptive to spirit and thus be able to hear it, feel it, and know it. We must be calm, peaceful, positive, and carrying a loving disposition (at the very least, to ourselves and, hopefully, to others). Often, I begin a session thinking to myself, "I am love, I am love." Since loving thoughts attract loving spirit, I am able to bring spirit closer to me.

We must be in a receptive state to connect with spirit. You might ask, "How can I possibly be in a more loving and receptive state with all the horrible things going on in the world these days and all the difficulties in my life?" My response to that question is *meditation,* which we'll discuss in more detail in the next chapter.

There are many examples of ways to calm down that tense and negatively biased mind of yours so you can allow yourself to create a loving mind. Take calm, peaceful walks in nature, which helps ground you. Listen to soft, soothing music or guided meditations. Take care of your body and mind by taking yoga classes or going to meditation studios. Sit and enjoy nature, like the steady rhythmic waves at a beach or the soft wind through the trees in a tall forest. Universal law states that Like Attracts Like. Spirit is love, and if we're loving, we can attract more loving spirit into our life and simultaneously become more aware of spirit all around us.

Perhaps you haven't been able to achieve that calm, loving state of being. We can't all be like Buddha, especially if we have a 9-to-5 job. So how can spirit get through to you then? If spirit has a compelling reason why they want to get your attention, then they can certainly do so. However, odds are that when spirit tried to make itself known to you in the past, you probably brushed it off as something else. Below is a list of potential experiences you may have had when spirit was trying to get your attention.

10 Ways Spirit Tries to Get Your Attention

1. **Tingling:** Have you ever felt inexplicable tingling sensations/goosebumps or cold/warm pockets of air on your body when the room isn't cold or hot? This is likely spirit's energy coming close to you or merging with you.
2. **Repeating numbers:** Do you often see unique numerical series everywhere you look (like 11:11; 12:12; or 1:11)? This is typically spirit or your spirit guides trying to get your attention or send you a message.
3. **Energy:** Have you ever just "felt" an energy or presence but can't explain it? High probability that's the energy of a spirit standing in your aura.
4. **Dog barks at empty space:** Has your dog ever barked incessantly at something in the house and appears to see something, but you don't see anything? Dogs have a strong sixth sense, and unlike humans they are more open to trusting. They also have far superior senses of sight, smell, and hearing that enable them to detect things we can't with our basic five senses. They may be barking at a spirit they can sense.
5. **Hearing your name when no one is present:** Have you ever heard your name or heard a sound and turned to look, but no one was there? More than likely, you clairaudiently heard the voice of a spirit calling your

name.

6. **Light flash:** Have you ever seen a flash of light out of the corner of your eye and turned to see what it was, but no one was there? After ruling out many of the common causes for this, odds may be high that spirit, often seen in balls of light, is present.
7. **Lights flickering:** Have the lights or a lamp in your home flickered on and off in an unusual way or turned on and off—and it's not just faulty wiring or a bulb? This is one of spirit's favorite ways to catch our attention, since electricity is energy and is something spirit can easily manipulate.
8. **Bizarre phone call:** Have you received a call on your cellphone from a number with all zeros (or it shows your loved one's phone number), and no one was on the line? Perhaps the phone often rings but only once. Spirit loves to play with electronics, since it is energy itself.
9. **Objects move independently:** Has an item in any room moved by itself without explanation? Using telekinesis, spirit can move objects by itself.
10. **Objects fall independently:** Has a book ever fallen off a shelf without explanation, whether you're present or before you got home? This is another example of telekinesis.

These are just a few examples of spirit making itself known in a noticeable way … even if you weren't looking for it. You don't have to be a practicing medium to contact spirit, for they're often connecting with us in surprising ways. Just because a loved one may not be with us in the physical doesn't mean they're not with us at all. As was written well over 2,000 years ago in the Bhagavad Gita 2;14-17, "The spirit is beyond destruction. No one can bring an end to the spirit which is everlasting." That's why I always say, "death is not goodbye."

9

Anyone Can Communicate With Spirit

"Everyone is born with psychic abilities. It's just a matter of knowing how to tap into it."
—Julien Offray de La Mettrie

Many people think the ability to contact spirit is some type of special "gift" bestowed upon a few select individuals in some magical way. People often believe those who can communicate with spirit must be unique, different, or special. Some less-than-scrupulous mediums may certainly give that impression or use that myth to their advantage. The truth is much less mystical.

Everyone has the innate ability to communicate with spirit, for we are all spirit residing in a human body for a set period of time. We are all souls endowed with the same capabilities. Each of us has the same basic psychic abilities, but most of us let them lie dormant. If you want to communicate with spirit, you must be fully open to spirit in all its manifestations, have a loving heart, and maintain a spiritual connection to the

Divine.

While we all have the ability to communicate with spirit, it does come easier to some and not others. Part of this comes from DNA, part from environment, and part from desire. This is the old *nature versus nurture* argument. The reality is the development of any medium combines both nature *and* nurture. The term *natural born medium* is somewhat misleading. It doesn't mean that a person can conduct clear spirit conversations without effort or training, because that's rare. It just means that their psychic gifts are closer to the surface, easier to access and more ready to train. Whether or not that person chooses to work on their gifts and adopt an appropriate mindset is up to them.

I'd compare this ability to great concert pianists learning how to play the piano. Everyone has the ability to play the piano. However, it comes easier to some than it does to others. Some people can learn to play the piano in an extraordinarily short amount of time and become fantastic in a very short time. This is partly due to innate skill and DNA. Conversely, others have to practice for what appears to be inordinate amounts of time to just master the basics, and thus easily become frustrated and often quit.

Some people can not only master the piano quickly, but they also have the passion and drive to practice so intensely that their ability to play the piano far surpasses everyone else. While it would appear that the greatest pianists are naturally gifted, the truth is that in addition to some innate ability, they are also more passionate, put in far more practice than others, rehearse over longer periods of time, and become substantially better players than their peers. In the end, the difference comes down to the amount of time put into training and practice to bring out the best of innate talents.

The same holds true for mediumship, as some of the most important elements of a medium's growth are training and practice, i.e. self-development. When I was just starting out, one of my mentors told me the way I could improve was through "practice, practice, and more practice!" Many of the top mediums today have been practicing their craft for thirty, forty, even fifty years, yet they say they're still learning. Spiritual medium and tutor Mavis Patilla, for example, has been practicing for fifty-four years. While most feel she is an expert medium, she says that she's learning new ways to improve her craft all the time.[15] The learning process never ends because we're always gaining new skills and broadening our repertoire.

It's important to realize that most spirits come to us with love and want only the best for us. While Hollywood loves to portray the spirit world as scary or evil, spirits are just regular people like us who formerly lived on earth. Now in spirit, they carry no ego and are significantly closer to loving Source energy. While most everyone is generally kind, you're always going to find some people who are not so nice, both on earth and the spirit world. Just as you wouldn't walk up to an ATM when you see a shady character lurking nearby, don't practice spirit communication when you or your surrounding atmosphere are emanating negative emotions.

As long as you work with loving thoughts, no so-called negative energy can interfere with you. Like attracts like. This is why you want to focus on loving energies with everything you do when you communicate with spirit. Pick your favorite higher spiritual being to work with, such as an angel, Jesus, Buddha, Mohammed, God, or whatever resonates with you.

Ask for them to surround you with their loving light. Set your intention to only speak with spirit that comes with the highest loving energy, and ask that spirit comes with the best intention for all those concerned. It's a universal law that spirit cannot interfere with your free will. So if you expressly state you only want to communicate with loving energies, that's all you'll connect with.

Some of the most readily available spirits who would love to communicate with you are your loved ones in spirit and your spirit guides. They may already be trying to contact you, but you just don't realize it yet. You may not even be open to it yet. We all tend be more skeptical of things we cannot see, touch, or readily prove. This skepticism grows as we move from childhood to adulthood.

For example, when we feel a sudden tingling or temperature change, we often chalk it up to something in our bodies or the room we're in. When something falls all by itself or we hear a strange noise when we're alone, we figure it was just the shifting of the house and not some unseen hand. When we see a quick flash or speck of light out the corner of our eye but see nothing when we turn that direction, we figure it was just a reflection or our imagination. I still do this. We may just be repeating what our parents told us when we were children. Spirit is always trying to get our attention, let us know they're still with us, communicate with us, and get us to open up to their very existence. It will do anything to accomplish that.

The Clairs

Everyone has nonphysical senses and psychic abilities. However, mediums have spent time and effort to develop them to a fine degree. Our five physical senses (touch, sight, smell, hearing, and taste) only help us detect things in the physical realm. To detect things in the nonphysical realm where spirit resides, we need to use our nonphysical or psychic senses. A medium works with what are referred to as the five primary "clairs," which is French for "clear."

The first psychic sense is *clairvoyance,* or the ability to see clearly in the mind's eye, without the aid of the physical eyes. This is often associated with the sixth chakra or the third eye chakra located in the front of the head between the eyebrows. Similar to one's imagination, this allows you to receive extrasensory impressions and symbols in the form of mental images through the mind's eye as if someone were playing a movie in your head or making images and symbols dance in specific ways so you could understand their meaning. I'm clairvoyant, and during readings I often see images in my mind, including remote views, that let me know what messages spirit is trying to convey.

You may be clairvoyant if you experience vivid dreams, visions, mental images, and mini-movies that flash into your inner awareness. You may be able to see the colors of the energy fields (auras) around people, plants, and animals, or perhaps you're able to see angels, ghosts, or other beings. You may have a propensity for clairvoyance if you're a "visual" person, can easily visualize solutions to problems, have a great sense of direction, or are very good with visual-spatial problems, like rearranging furniture or loading and arranging the items in the dishwasher.

The second clair is *clairsentience,* or clear-feeling. This is the ability to receive intuitive messages via feelings or emotions. You have a "gut feeling" or "something doesn't feel right," and you experience it viscerally, as a physical sensation, in your body. For example, during a reading I may have a strong feeling that I need to start speaking about a certain topic the spirit wants me to discuss, or say something very specific because I feel it is very important to the sitter. On other occasions, I'll feel a discomfort at the area where the spirit person had a disease or was injured, which lets me know the cause of their passing.

People with clairsentience *feel* the experience of other people's emotions, ailments or injuries. They can also feel the physical and emotional pain of a land or a place where tragic events have occurred; these sensations can manifest as fear, jealousy, insecurity, hatred, or pain. An example of this is a gifted psychic medium who gets an upset stomach when negative entities are nearby or are pestering one of her clients.

The third clair is *clairaudience,* or clear-hearing. This is a way of receiving messages and detecting sounds without using physical ears and is associated with the fifth Chakra or the throat chakra. A medium can often hear songs or phrases with their clairaudience that carry a meaning to the sitter, but they are sounds that others don't hear using their physical ears. Occasionally during readings, I'll hear short portions of songs or phrases I know, the lyrics of which have meaning to the sitter.

Someone is clairaudient if they mainly receive their intuitive information with their inner or outer hearing. Yes, we're talking about hearing voices! An example is that you're driving to work and suddenly hear, "Take the next exit." There is no one in the vehicle with you. However, the message was clear, and seemed to come from outside of yourself. You take the next exit instead of driving your usual route. When you arrive at work, you learn you avoided a five-car pileup, which would have made you miss a very important meeting. You might lean toward clairaudience if you are naturally attuned to sounds, tones, rhythm, and music. If you sing, play music, have an easy time remembering voices, or can easily hear it in someone's voice when they're lying to you, then you might be clairaudient.

The fourth clair is *claircognizance,* or clear-knowing. Claircognizance is the ability to suddenly know something without logic or facts. It's like a stroke of instant insight or a download of information that needs no processing or interpretation. It may help to think of it as an inner knowing.

Claircognizance can be experienced as a nagging idea or unrelenting thought, much like the persistent awareness that someone is lying to you when you have no physical evidence of it. Many individuals confuse claircognizance (clear-knowing) with clairempathy (clear-emotion) or clairsentience (clear-feeling) because their "knowing" is quickly followed by either a personal emotional or physical reaction to the insight. Over time, paying attention to how the insight comes into your awareness will help you distinguish the difference. Additionally, some confuse clairaudience with claircognizance, since a person can suddenly become aware of a song and begin to think they are hearing internally rather than just knowing the song suddenly.

Two other psychic senses that are a bit less common include *clairalience,* or clear-smelling, and *clairgustance,* or clear-tasting. With clairalience, you could be sitting in a room and suddenly begin smelling you father's unique tobacco smoke, yet no one in the room is smoking a pipe. In a reading, I once had an overpowering sense of a bakery smell with fresh bread baking. This was a piece of evidence the sitter's father, who was a baker, wanted to get across to her. Clairgustance is the sudden sensation that you're tasting something in your mouth, yet you're not eating anything. That taste could remind you of your grandmother's unique apple pie, and that's all it would take to recognize that she was right there trying to communicate with you.

Meditation—Sitting in the Silence and Sitting in the Power

Intention and focus are two important attributes for spirit communication. You need a positive and loving intention to attract only the spirits with highest vibrations and loving attitude. With this approach, protection is rarely needed because a loving intention has already been set forth into the universe. Focus is important so that you pay attention to every piece of information you receive and don't ignore it.

Additionally, during your reading you may begin losing the power that fuels your connection, causing you to lose your focus and link with spirit. This is much like when a radio station is not fully focused or tuned to a radio frequency and you hear a mix of static and chatter. As a result, the signal is garbled and difficult to understand. If you have lost your power, then spirit's signal will seem garbled and unintelligible.

Meditation is a good tool to improve your ability to focus and strengthen your link with spirit. This helps you calm down and empty your mind, while eliminating the constant chatter going on inside your head. Also, as you chant mantras during meditations, you naturally become more focused on what you are chanting. You can get the same focus if you concentrate on visualizing an object. The more you meditate, the better your focus, which will in turn help you clear your mind. Consequently, once you have a clear canvas on which to paint, spirit will more easily be able to "paint" its information for you to see.

One meditation you should begin with is called "Sitting in the Silence," which will help you increase your focus and help clear your mind. Try to sit for this meditation for fifteen minutes every day.

Sitting in the Silence

1. First, sit and relax in a comfortable, straight-backed chair, feet on the floor, with your hands laying comfortably on your legs, palms up in a receiving fashion.
2. Begin to calm your breathing and focus your attention on your inhalations and exhalations. This can be done with eyes open or shut. Do this for several minutes until your breath becomes slow and relaxed.
3. Ask your spirit helpers for loving protection or just think thoughts of loving kindness. Envision love surrounding you and protecting you in a beautiful bubble of protection. You can also say a prayer that is meaningful to you, either aloud or to yourself. Do whatever makes you feel safe and full of love and joy.
4. In your mind's eye, imagine a tall, white candle with a flame that has just been lit. Focus your attention on the

flame. Look at how it flickers, how it moves from side to side, how it subtly changes shape and slightly changes color. Look at the interior part of the flame, with a cool blue oval at the base of the wick. Move up and see a white-hot flame. Surrounding the flame on either side is the hint of a soft orange aura.

5. Continue focusing on this flame for fifteen minutes and empty your mind of all its clutter as you think about nothing but the flame. Watch it flicker and change shape over time. It's normal if extraneous thoughts enter your mind. When this occurs, just allow them to leave as easily as they entered. Bring your focus back to the flame.
6. At the end of the meditation, slowly bring your awareness back to the room. Become aware of your fingers and your toes. Wiggle your fingers and toes, firstly gently and then more quickly. Once you feel more grounded, slowly open your eyes and realize you have returned. Welcome back.
7. Upon completion of the meditation you should feel more empowered. The meditation enables your soul to rise to the surface so it can remember what its purpose is in this incarnation.

To best improve your readings, you should do another meditation that enables spirit to see and work with your mind, sharpen your focus, and increase your spirituality. Try to do this daily for fifteen minutes in the beginning, and later increase the meditation time to thirty minutes. This meditation is called "Sitting in the Power" and expands on the "Sitting in the Silence" meditation.

Sitting in the Power

1. First, sit and relax in a comfortable, straight-backed chair with your hands on your legs, palms up in a receiving fashion.
2. Begin to calm your breathing and focus your attention on your inhalations and exhalations. Do this for several minutes until your breath becomes slow and relaxed. You can ask your spirit helpers for loving protection or you can just think thoughts of loving kindness that surrounds you and protects you in a beautiful bubble of protection. You can also say a prayer that is meaningful to you. Do whatever makes you feel safe and full of love.
3. Next, after you are calm and focused, bring your attention to your heart space and see in your mind's eye a small ball of soft, glowing white light. As you focus your attention there, notice the white light begin to brighten and grow and react to your breath.
4. With each exhalation, feel as though you are blowing up a balloon and further expanding your white light with each breath. In this way you will finally fill up your chest space, and subsequently your arms, head, midsection, and legs.
5. See this white light slowly expand to fill your entire body. Realize this bright white light filling your interior is actually your glowing spirit, which exists within you.
6. Your white light of spirit has no boundaries, so you can see it easily expand beyond your body. First, let it fill your aura. Then, allow it to fill the entire room in which you sit. Your white light continues to grow and soon surrounds the globe.

7. Next, send a beam of loving, white light from your spirit up to the heavens to reach out for the spirit world.
8. As your light expands out, you are met halfway by the Love That Knows No Bounds in a ray of golden light that comes to you from the heavens to tenderly envelop your entire being with love and encircle you, protect you, and empower you. You are overcome with bliss, the likes of which you have never known, and an unconditional, divine love that is all-encompassing and all-accepting.
9. Feel your entire body begin to tingle with warm, loving energy and know that you are loved by spirit.
10. Thank spirit for this beautiful meeting between two worlds, and feel the joy and happiness that wells up inside you. As you do, start thinking about your Joy Guide and ask to meet them. Your joy and happiness and love will attract your Joy Guide to you. Begin to imagine what your Joy Guide might look like (this stimulates your creative mind and clairvoyance), and you may be able to feel or see them if they chose to reveal themselves to you.
11. Stay in this blissful feeling for as long as you would like.
12. At the end of the meditation, slowly bring your awareness back to the room. Become aware of your fingers and your toes. Wiggle your fingers and toes, firstly gently and then more quickly. Once you feel more grounded, slowly open your eyes and realize you have returned.
13. If you don't meet your guides on your first sitting, that's totally normal and quite fine, so don't get upset. Just keep trying to meet them with this meditation. Once you are in a good mindset and they are ready, you two will meet. Just always be in a loving frame of mind, for love attracts positive spirit.

We spiritual beings living in temporary physical shells can communicate with our spirit brothers and sisters. We just need to expand our minds so we can not only understand their presence but also learn how to communicate with them. This is a process that requires time, hard work, persistence, patience, and, most of all, desire. While this is not easy, the end result of communicating with spirit and hearing their loving messages is well worth the effort.

10

Communication Concepts

"Wise men speak because they have something to say."
— Plato

Entire books have been written and advanced courses developed about the intricate mechanics of mediumship, which is beyond the scope of this book. These are more appropriate for people seeking detailed knowledge of mediumship to improve their own practice. However, I thought it would be helpful to briefly describe some of the basic concepts concerning spirit communication for the merely curious. If you are searching for a greater understanding of your natural gifts, this chapter may serve as an overview to aid in your exploration.

Arguably the most important concept to consider as you begin your exploration is motive. Why do you want to be a medium? If you approach mediumship from a spiritual perspective, you will be able to help many more people and have an easier time developing your abilities, and you'll do no harm. The right reasons for being a medium will help you sustain the effort required to learn the practice and help others in need. These reasons include serving others (sitters, mankind, spirit people), fulfilling a calling (helping, comforting, healing), looking to touch souls, making a difference in the world, and demonstrating spiritual truths and the survival of the soul. Your motive should feel like a passion or burning desire. This will keep you going through all the difficult and frustrating times.

Unfortunately, some people seek to become mediums for the wrong reasons. If any of these are your own reasons, they may hinder your progress and wind up hurting recipients. Inappropriate motives include fame, fortune, power, control, praise, feeding your ego, and feeling important. Not only could these cause harm, but they're not spiritual or sacred. This totally conflicts with the fundamental precept of mediumship as a sacred ability. Furthermore, these internal drivers won't sustain you during the inevitable times when you become frustrated and just feel like quitting.

To develop your mediumship, you should understand the three equally important components involved: *theory, practice,* and *self-development.* The development journey is a lifetime of work, since there's always more information to learn and more abilities to unfold. Because you will have ups and down or trials and tribulations, you need patience, perseverance, and, above all, commitment. While the experience is wonderfully rewarding, you need to build a proper foundation.

Theory

It's vital to learn the theory and fundamentals of mediumship before you move to the next steps. The understanding that the theory provides makes it easier for students to practice and achieve better results. Many people want to launch straight into communicating with spirit before they really understand what they're doing. That's similar to trying to drive a car without learning how to drive or understanding a car's controls. You wouldn't get far without going off the road. To successfully maintain a link with spirit and deliver good evidence, you need to have a solid understanding of what spirit communication truly is, how it works, and what you need to do.

You should take many classes and workshops in an effort to broaden your abilities and understanding. There are many offered by local Spiritualist churches and mediums, as well as online courses. In my opinion, the most comprehensive and reasonably priced course has been constructed by well-known teaching medium Martin Twycross, CSNU. This excellent course, titled "A Course in Mediumship Study Program," contains a series of twenty-four teaching videos and tutorials along with a detailed home study program. It covers the theoretical foundations and the mechanics and workings of mediumship, and helps you develop mediumship to a high standard. The course is appropriate for beginners but also offers training for more advanced mediums seeking to further their knowledge. Given its in-depth and broad-based coverage, I believe this would be a great way for you to progress if you are just beginning your journey.

Evidential mediumship is, at its core, a connection to the spirit realm via a person who has developed psychic senses, the power to raise their awareness, and a clear purpose in a structured format. Mediumship is an active process: it's a two-way communication between spirit and the living. The more you realize that you're actually conversing with real people who are still alive on the other side, the more complete a discussion you'll have with the spirit person. This encourages you to become more flexible with the information you're seeking. Just have a natural conversation with spirit.

This mental conversation requires a tremendous amount of energy. In my readings, I tell clients that mediumship is a three-way energy cocktail between spirit, the medium, and the sitter. It requires a great deal of positive and loving energy to raise the vibrations high enough to create a strong link between spirit and the medium. Another somewhat similar analogy I often use is that of a mobile phone, which requires a powerful battery with lots of energy to pull in a weak signal. Likewise with mediumship, you need a tremendous amount of mental energy to establish a link with spirit and receive a clear communication. With love as the strongest emotion and most positive energy, this creates the strongest link.

Many think that mediumship is a passive activity, similar to meditation, because it allows the mind to be calm and open, without any conscious activity. When I was starting out on my journey, I also thought this was the correct method, since that's how I seemed to get all my information. I just sat there and allowed spirit to impress on me different images, feelings, and words. The only problem was that I received random information. The communication had no structure, no cohesiveness, and no consistency. Nevertheless, the information coming through was unique and extremely colorful, providing no doubt who the spirit was.

Practice

I soon learned that I should actively ask questions of spirit, and do so in a structured format to get specific pieces of evidence and guide the conversation. I discovered there was a system I could follow and use repeatedly for every reading. However, no sooner did I discover this system than I encountered a problem with my development. I found some teachers insisted I only use an overly strict and limiting approach to evidentiary information. This stemmed from a traditional Spiritualist approach to spirit communication. Furthermore, I felt that my conscious mind began to interfere as I tried to ask a long list of questions.

As I advanced through my development, I eventually discovered the best readings were a combination of the structured format together with unrestricted information that I allowed spirit to offer me. I found that by going beyond the limiting shopping list, which painted only a silhouette, I could describe the spirit person back to life in 3-D by allowing the spirit to speak freely about itself, much the way I did in my early days. I figured out that I needed to use the list of questions as a starting point, but I also needed to encourage spirit to tell me what *it* wanted me to know. This way spirit could tell me how I could best describe it.

Using C.E.R.T. to Structure a Reading

The most fundamental and perhaps well-known system used to structure a reading has the acronym C.E.R.T., which stands for *contact, evidence, reason,* and *tie-it-up.*

Start with a *contact* by linking with spirit. You can do this by setting your intention with a prayer, slowing and expanding your breathing, visualizing your love expanding, and stating positive affirmations. Clear your mind, perhaps by focusing on the flame of a candle. Envision the spirit person's hand on your shoulder or in your hands. Invite spirit to gather near and blend with you. Describe everything you're receiving from spirit in detail. Give what you get, and don't leave anything out. The evidence and meaning is often found in the details. Offering the details of the communication prevents you from misinterpreting what you're receiving or leaving out critical information that might be relevant for the recipient.

Next, ask spirit to give you *evidence* and information about itself. Most beginning mediums are taught to work with a list of questions to gather unique details about the spirit communicator in a structured manner. These details might include gender, age, cause of passing, relationship to sitter, personality, character, profession, hobbies, unique physical features or markings, descriptions of clothing they wore, special items of interest and shared memories, and proof of the living mind such as spirit sharing recent events in your life. Think of this as a shopping list you can use for each reading.

Ask the spirit why it has come to communicate with the recipient. Learn the *reason* the spirit has come, which usually is a message for the sitter. Often the spirit person wants to express its love to the sitter, apologize for actions that may have caused harm to those in the physical or relay a regret it has about its life on earth or choices it made while here.

Finally, *tie up* the reading by asking the sitter if they have any questions, after which you can let them know the reading has come to an end.

My suggestion to you is that once you are able to proficiently gather details from your shopping list of questions without even thinking, you should expand beyond this skeletal description. This will help you truly paint spirit back to life in all their glory. Ask spirit, "How might I best describe you?" You may find you will start getting some very colorful and unique pieces of information. In this manner you will be able to really describe spirit's story beyond just a cookie-cutter format, enabling the recipient to fully acknowledge spirit's presence.

When you communicate with spirit, you need to surrender fully to them so you can receive everything they are sending you. It should feel like you are opening completely and disconnecting from your personal mind. Project yourself into the spirit world, become spirit, and blend your soul together with theirs. This will open the door for them to relay feelings, emotions, pictures, and sounds to you.

Invite spirit to merge their soul with yours so that they lightly overshadow you, enabling you to feel their feelings, pick up their mannerisms, see them closely, and know things they know. Surrender to the feelings you receive and the light overshadowing of spirit. You must trust everything you receive and go with your first instinct, no matter how unusual or odd it may seem, even if you don't understand it. Always remember the phrase "Trust and Surrender." Spirit knows what it's doing and how it wants to get across specific information.

Often the information you receive may make no sense to you, but it may have meaning to the sitter. Remember, always give what you receive and share everything as you perceive it, without interpretation. Also, don't be afraid of getting a no from the sitter. You could just be misinterpreting the information rather than giving it directly as you received it. Or perhaps another spirit is stepping in with different information, which will confuse the flow of the reading.

Problems in communication often crop up when you allow your analytical mind to creep back in during the reading. You might receive a piece of information and think, "That's too bizarre, so it's probably just my imagination." This is your analytical mind taking over. Don't analyze what you're saying. Don't judge the value of the information or compare your work or yourself to other mediums. You are the instrument for spirit to relay their messages, so keep your focus on spirit. You are having a conversation with spirit, so have fun and enjoy it.

The Gift of a Development Circle

Once you understand what mediumship is and how it works, the next step is to find somewhere to practice under the guidance of a good teacher, like at a weekly development circle. These are often held at Spiritualist churches or are run by local mediums and some are also on line. I don't think I can emphasize enough how important weekly development circles are, as they allow you to practice in the safety of your own group without pressure, enable you to receive guidance from the teacher in circle, and give you a sense of consistency, not to mention the camaraderie and support of fellow mediums.

One of the most important parts of my development was sitting in a development circle near me run by Lee VanZyl, founder of the Montclair Psychic School. Lee not only taught me the fundamentals of spirit communication in her workshops, but she helped me unfold my abilities by practicing in her circle every week. I started out like a lump of clay, but every week she and other tutors helped me improve with their helpful suggestions and guidance. Lee is like a master potter who turns clay into beautiful works of art.

When I first started in her circle, I carried an inferiority complex and thought I didn't belong because there were so many people present who had much more experience than I did. But it was this diverse mix of levels that also spurred me to grow as I learned from the more experienced practitioners. I saw what they were doing, so I tried to replicate it. When it worked, I added it to my repertoire. Likewise, when Lee would suggest I try something that worked, I included it in my tool kit. The development circle also represented a practice arena in which I could stretch myself and test out new methods of connecting with spirit.

Importantly, Lee always said to step out of my comfort zone so that I'd continue to grow. She also wanted me to set a goal of becoming better than her. Lee believed that if she could get her students to surpass her, that meant she had taught them well. That's the mark of a great teacher. So far we're all trying to surpass her, but we have a long way to go. Like anything worthwhile, it takes a great deal of time, effort, and practice to develop mediumship to an excellent standard where you can serve others.

Take as many opportunities to practice as you can. Don't be in a rush to develop quickly, but give yourself time to allow your gifts to unfold at a steady pace. Most people feel it requires several years of steady practice and devoted study to raise your mediumship to a high caliber. Mediumship is a journey of continued unfoldment.

Self-Development

The third component to developing mediumship is self-development. While you can learn the mechanics underlying the process, communicating with spirit is first and foremost a spiritual and sacred process. The key to unfolding your gifts is creating the right spiritual conditions for them to unfold. Self-development practices include meditation, prayer, and dealing with any personal issues or emotional baggage that may hold you back or block spirit from working clearly with you.

Meditation

Meditation practices are the foundation for developing high quality mediumship. One of the reasons I had my spiritual awakening and numerous subsequent encounters with spirit early in my journey was because I had developed a daily meditation practice, with some sessions lasting up to an hour. This helped me learn to relax and still my chaotic, stress-filled mind. One of the hardest lessons for trainee mediums to learn is how to stay focused and discipline their minds to leave behind their own personal problems. Therefore daily meditation, even for only ten minutes, is critical.

A fundamental element to successful mediumship is the ability to expand and strengthen your energy field with meditation, which is similar to charging a battery. The meditation called "Sitting in the Power," described earlier, does just that by expanding the power within the medium's auric field. Spirit uses the aura as a connection vehicle to connect to the medium and blend with their soul. The more you can merge with spirit, the clearer the descriptions and the greater the evidential information will be.

The stronger the medium's energy field is, the greater the ability to sustain the link and receive good evidence from the spirit world. Building the power and sustaining it is a skill that trainee mediums should learn early in their development, as it can make a significant improvement to the rate of their development. Many tutors suggest "Sitting in the Power" several times a week for ten to thirty minutes per session.

Developing mediumship is about spiritualizing the self. Perhaps most importantly, you should learn how to grow spiritually, improve your relationship with the Divine, and focus on the love in your heart. Key attributes needed to develop mediumship include love, commitment, a desire to serve, sensitivity, an open mind, and the ability to trust. You can only go so far with learning the theory and fundamentals of mediumship. *The real key to unlocking your mediumship is your own self and spiritual development.* Really, all development is self-development because it's a journey that has to be undertaken by you. Nobody else can do it for you. Mediumship is one of the most wonderful and fulfilling journeys there is. Take the time to explore it and enjoy it.

If you're interested in developing your own mediumship, I'd love to help you. You can explore my school of mediumship here: **MontClairMedium School of Psychic Arts**.

Many thanks to Martin Twycross for his significant contribution to this chapter.[16]

11

How To Get The Best From A Mediumship Reading

"Ask and you will receive, and your joy will be complete."
—John 16:24 (*NIV*)

When people sit for a reading with me, I find they often don't understand the process of spirit communication or how spirit works. Sometimes they're quite skeptical and are just waiting for the reading to fail. Other times they only believe the experience is real if they hear a code word or hear from one specific person. All this negativity dampens a medium's ability to connect, and the sitter has a poor experience.

Try to think of it from the spirit's point of view for a second. As a spirit, you have finally found a medium you can work with and are just as excited to get your message through to your loved one on earth as they are to hear from you. After all, you're still quite alive on the other side, and you're just jumping at the chance to speak to your loved one here. Can you imagine how you would feel if your loved one on earth said, "Nah, I don't believe it's you."

It takes a tremendous amount of positive energy between the medium, the sitter, and the spirit to make the connection work well. The higher and more loving the vibrations from those in the physical, the stronger and clearer the communication will be. I find the recipient can act much like an energetic battery that provides power for the session. Additionally, since this is a connection to the spiritual, deep reverence for the process and prayers are quite appropriate.

The best way to approach a mediumistic session is to come with an open mind, a loving heart, and no expectations for what should happen. The sitter should keep his or her arms and legs uncrossed to foster a positive, open attitude. Spirit will never disappoint us and will often come to us in the most astounding ways. They will give us proof they are still with us and can still see us, hear our thoughts, and approve of our decisions; they may ask for forgiveness, but above all they will share how much they love us. Spirit learns profound lessons on the other side and sees existence in completely new ways.

When you go to a reading, there are fairly standard expectations you should have. For example, a well-trained and experienced medium will provide a highly structured reading. He or she may begin by describing the mediumship process and offering some basic instructions for the reading. The medium might then offer a prayer or statement of intention before launching into the reading itself. After a brief pause to get a strong connection with spirit, the well-trained medium will provide evidential details about the spirit who is present.

These details, which we discussed in the last chapter, should account for the majority of the reading. Toward the end of the reading, the medium will relay a few messages from spirit. These might include that person's love for you, or perhaps an apology. Spirit might ask for forgiveness or indicate approval for some decision. At the end of the session, the experienced medium will answer any questions you might have and then end the reading.

A good evidential medium will never ask for information other than confirmation of what they're receiving with a simple yes, no, or maybe. Mediums are supposed to *give* information, not ask for it. If the medium begins to ask too many questions, as if they seem to be fishing for information, just respond with yes/no/maybe answers to avoid this. While a medium may ask too many questions, it doesn't necessarily mean they're a fraud, however. It probably means they haven't been properly trained. Furthermore, as a sitter you should never volunteer information. As the saying goes, "Don't feed the medium." A good medium sets out about 75 percent of his information as a way to build evidence and display the existence and continuity of life. Only the final 25 percent will be a message from spirit. The message should not be confused with the evidence.

You should expect evidence to be incontrovertible, unique to the person in spirit, and something the medium would have no way of knowing. Also, don't make the information fit, since there are no such things as "near misses." For example, if the medium says he has a spirit person with a white four-legged animal that seems like a large dog, don't say, "I can take that since my dad had a white cat." The evidence has to clearly match what you know. In other words, don't give a yes answer when it really should be a maybe answer. In fact, by making the information fit, you may remove the opportunity for more meaningful evidence and connection by using that information to mean something different and less meaningful.

Incontrovertible Evidence

One example of incontrovertible evidence is if the medium brings through information that your deceased father approves of what you have done with his old den, goes on to describe the den and all the changes you made in detail, yet you know the medium never could have known anything about that den. *That* is evidence of proof of the living mind and that spirit is still with you. Just saying "Your father sees that you did something in the house and he likes it" without accurate detail is definitely not evidence. This is vague and could be applied to many people. You should always demand the more strict, detailed, and unique evidential information from the medium. Spirit has lots of tricks up its sleeves to get its evidence through.

Another issue I encounter is sitters who only want to hear from one special person. If they don't hear from that person, then they feel the reading is a failure. That's the kind of negative energy that disrupts the delicate flow of the reading and can cause the energy to sag. This makes any connection weak, distant, and difficult to work with. The desired person may not come through due to spirit's own reasons. Sometimes they're just not ready. Maybe they're learning to communicate or acclimating to a new environment, or they're busy doing something else. Possibly they see the sitter is not ready. You can't demand a spirit person show up at a set time or place any more than you can a living person.

A similar issue holds true with code words. Just because you want your dearly departed to reveal your secret code word doesn't mean they will. If the medium has brought through a tremendous amount of evidential information, yet you don't get the secret code word, don't count the entire session as a bust. Look at the reading comprehensively, for it was probably very good. However, too many sitters set themselves up for disappointment by putting such a high bar on the reading that it's quite easy to miss the expectation.

While it's good to be cautious of people who prey on the emotions of the bereaved, try not to close down so much that you close the energy for the reading itself. You-the-sitter are a vital piece of the energetic puzzle and should try to contribute to building the sacred energy so you can hear all the loving pieces of information and healing that spirit has to offer. In the final analysis, a reading is really spirit's effort to send love, comfort, and healing to their loved one who remains on earth. It's this reading that can transform a sitter and enable them to live their life to the fullest again, especially if they were grieving.

Below I outline several helpful points that should assist you in getting the most from your session and giving you the best experience possible.

1. **Fill Your Heart with Love and Positive Vibrations.** Since spirit exists at a much higher vibration compared to us in the physical, we need to raise our vibrations substantially to meet spirit halfway and establish contact. The highest vibration possible is love and forgiveness toward others, similar to what Jesus Christ and Buddha taught. Together with joy and enthusiasm, feelings of love will create the ideal conditions of high vibrations for communication. Uncross your arms and legs to stay open to spirit. Display any negativity and the spiritual call gets disconnected. If you come to a session in a highly emotional state (terribly upset, depressed, angry, influenced by drugs or alcohol) then that negative energy will either squelch or block the completion of the

spirit's connection with the medium.

2. **Be Open to Whatever Happens.** Your loved ones in spirit and spirit guides work hard together to get in contact with you through a medium with whom they can work well. Often, they influence your decision of the medium you will ultimately seek out for a reading. Since spirit knows best what you need for your growth and it directs the communication, you may be surprised at who comes through in the reading and what their message is. While the love between you and a certain spirit may be particularly strong, don't be shocked if someone else comes through instead. This doesn't negate their love for you, nor should it imply anything negative about you.

3. **Take Notes, or Record Your Session.** Often you may receive information from spirit that you can't immediately place or understand. Since spirit often communicates with the medium using symbols that could have multiple meanings, it sometimes becomes a game of charades and an effort to figure out what the clues mean. No symbol or image given by spirit is ever wasted, as spirit is extremely efficient. Take notes or record the session so you can later think about the information that you can't initially understand. Also, spirit may give information that other family members know but you don't. Go back to your family and ask if they recognize the evidence. In other situations, spirit sometimes provides information about something that hasn't happened yet, but it wants you to know and be prepared in advance. This is another reason why it's so important to be open to whatever you receive.

4. **Invite Your Spirit Guides and Loved Ones to Join You.** Thoughts, intentions, and emotions are incredibly powerful.

In fact, these are the most powerful energies in the spirit world. If you invite your spirit guides, angels, and loved ones to join you at the reading, confirm for them that you will be there for the stated date, time, and place of the session. Think of it as a spiritual party invitation that when sent with love will often receive a good response. Again, don't demand or expect anyone to appear, but the sheer intention will have a very positive impact.

5. **Don't Get Upset if a Specific Loved One Doesn't Come Through.** Sometimes spirit determines that it is in your best interest for maximum spiritual growth to hear from one person but not another, so don't have your heart set on one specific person coming through. If you're so set on hearing from one person, you might just block all communication from anyone. Additionally, it is possible the person you're waiting for may not be ready to communicate yet. Either they recently arrived and they haven't learned how to properly communicate, or they may still be resting from a traumatic experience that brought them to spirit. Additionally, spirit may determine that you aren't ready to hear from someone yet.

6. **Only Respond with "Yes,"" No," or" "Maybe" Answers.** Never give a medium any information about yourself or your loved ones either in advance or during the session. Spirit wants to demonstrate its continued existence by providing volumes of evidence to you through the medium so that you believe your loved ones are still around you. The best way to enable this demonstration by spirit is by only responding to evidential information with answers of yes, no, or maybe. This also prevents feeding the medium too much information. If the medium begins to ask open-ended questions, it's possible

he or she is starting to fish for clues. This is an absolute no-no in mediumistic circles.

7. **Let the Medium Do Their Job.** Don't disrupt the session by asking a list of questions or becoming argumentative or interrupting the flow of the reading. Some people have come to a session only to bombard the medium with endless questions and expecting answers. It's okay to ask some questions at the end for clarification or follow-up, but you came for a reading to hear from your loved ones in spirit. Let the medium do their job so you can.

8. **Come Relaxed, and Pay Attention.** Perhaps the best thing you can do in preparation for a session is to meditate as well as pray to your loved ones in spirit or your spirit guides or even the Divine Spirit. This helps calm your busy mind, brings harmony, reduces stress and anxiety, opens your pathways to love and forgiveness, and raises your vibrations so you help establish clear spirit communication. You will also be more alert so you can think more clearly, be in the moment, and provide better responses. In this loving and relaxed state of mind, almost anything is possible, and you improve your chances for having a wonderful and meaningful mediumship session.

I hope these ideas help you get the best from your next mediumship session. Connecting with spirit is a beautiful and magical experience and something in which everyone should be able to participate.

III

What Does Spirit Want Us To Know?

12

Spirit Does Remember Us After Their Transition

"In my life I find that memories of the spirit linger and sweeten long after memories of the brain have faded."
—Harry Connick Jr.

I'm often asked if a spirit remembers us after a person dies. It seems a common misconception that when a person dies, their spirit goes off into some faraway existence, never to return or have contact with us ever again. The reality is quite different.

We are spirit temporarily living in a physical shell. When a person passes into the spirit world, the only thing that disintegrates and falls away is the physical body. Everything else remains intact, including a person's consciousness and their memory. Spirit remembers us because of the love we shared when we were together in the physical. The love shared between two people—whether spouses or family members or close friends—is the special energy that tightly bonds us together forever.

Consequently, we remain in the thoughts of our loved ones

in spirit regardless of their state of evolution—just as they stay in ours. They also visit us more often than we realize. In fact, the more time and experience spirit gains in the afterlife, the greater their appreciation for everyone and everything that was in their physical life. When a person passes on, he or she doesn't just immediately leave behind the past life and loved ones on earth. There is a gradual period of learning and progression that spirit people experience, which keeps their awareness open to the earth plane.

Recipients sometimes ask me after a reading, "Does he still love me and watch over me?" I can unequivocally say yes. After spirit delivers all of its evidence, it always mentions how much it loves us, whether directly or through an apology for something it did that hurt us. Spirit often impresses upon me that it keeps watch over its loved ones still here on earth. People often forget that spirit isn't floating around somewhere "up there" in the clouds. In fact, it's right here with us; but because its vibration is so much greater than that of our dense physical bodies, we can't detect it with our five main senses.

Vibrations and Elevations

Without giving it much thought, the idea that spirit lands exist far away would seem to make sense because a spirit that is a high vibration being must logically be in a higher elevation. We've all seen paintings with angels flying up in the clouds, and heard or read from religious texts that heaven is up in the sky with God. So it seems logical that high vibration spirits must also be up there with the angels. However, vibration and elevation are not necessarily related.

Vibration rates, which are the speed at which particles oscillate or move back and forth, have nothing to do with elevation, which is the height of an object above a given level. I'll refer back to the example of the spinning fan blade I made in Chapter 4. A fan could be standing right next to us with its blades spinning at hyper speeds that are so fast we can't see it. The blades may be invisible to our eyes, but they are still by our side, not up in the clouds. Thus, there is no correlation between vibration and elevation.

The same can be said for spirit and the spirit world. They exist at extremely high vibration rates, just like the fan spinning at hyper speeds. However, like the fan blade, the unseen spirit world still exists and remains close to our side. Spirit has often said that distance is a human construct in the physical world and has no bearing to them in their nonphysical existence, and they do agree that they remain by our side in an alternate reality.

During the presentation of evidence to the sitter, for example, spirit will often show it is still with us by giving memories of events that were shared with the recipient. This is done as a way of saying "Remember when we did this?" More impressively, spirit also presents memories of events it has seen *after* it has passed, which is done as a form of proof of survival. It may share memories of a daughter's wedding, or the birth of a child, or a birthday or a special anniversary party, all witnessed after it died. These can be some of the most impactful pieces of evidence, as they clearly display that our loved ones are fully alive on the other side and are watching over us and seeing what we are doing.

Nevertheless, many people believe that when a person dies, they no longer exist anywhere and are no longer alive in any form. This can be due to religious upbringing, strict religious beliefs, or their skeptical nature. This is often true with younger adults who know fewer people who have passed on. Additionally, many younger adults tend to be more skeptical by nature as they are still charting their path in life, and they want things to be tangible and matter of fact. Unfortunately, spirit and spirit communication does not offer those qualities. The best spirit can do is offer countless pieces of incontrovertible and unique evidence, most of which could never have been known by the medium. Yet even then, belief still rests on a certain "knowingness" that there are other powers in the universe beyond what we can see and touch.

People in spirit are still real people—alive and well, just without a physical body. They have spirit bodies and are quite active, learning and expanding their abilities and ways to help others. The one time they may encounter struggles with their expanding awareness is when their loved ones on earth remain in extreme or extended mourning, as this catches the attention of the spirit person and may pull them back to earth, slowing their progression.

Grief

Grief is a natural part of the mourning process. However, spirit has detailed in automatic writings that when grief becomes too extreme or extended, it creates a purple cord that binds that mourner with the deceased. The person in spirit feels that emotional tug, and if the mourner's emotions are strong enough, this will actually pull the spirit back to the earth plane as it tries to console the mourner in grief. This is one way that spirits may become earth-bound; they would rather stay on the physical plane in an effort to console their loved one on earth. This interferes with the spirit's growth and progression to higher levels.

So while it's wonderful to know that spirit is quite aware of how we feel and tries to console us in our grief, we should remember that the spirit person is now actually quite happy, feels no pain, and is expanding their consciousness. We shouldn't be sad about their departure; we should be happy for them because they've finally reached a world where love is the fabric of their existence and the pain of physical living has passed. This is what the spirit world is all about—love and joy.

Love and Joy in the Spirit World

Both NDE accounts and automatic writings from spirit authors depict similar information about this love and joy in the spirit world. They also support my experience during my reawakening. Love is unconditional, all-encompassing and fully accepting. We are loved just for existing, and we are perfect beings, for good and bad are merely figments of the human ego mind. This is not a romantic love; it is a parental and brotherly love. The ultimate love is from God who provides His Divine Love as the father.

Brotherly love stems from the idea that in fact there is no separation, only unity, and that we are all one universal consciousness. This is what Jesus was referring to as he commanded us to "Love your neighbor as yourself." He said this because in essence our neighbor is us—there is no separation, so if we love our neighbor, we will in turn be loving ourselves. Everything in existence has the same energy coursing through it: Source energy, or chi, from tai chi or qigong, or ki from Reiki, or prana or mana. It's all the same energy, and it exists everywhere simultaneously. As a result, we are all one, and to love another is to love our self.

13

Love Is The Answer

"To see the universal and all pervading Spirit of Truth face to face, one must be able to love the meanest of all creation as oneself."
—Mahatma Gandhi

Why would spirit expend so much energy trying to get its messages back to us when it's living in an idyllic and peaceful world now? The answer to that question is simple and comes down to one word: love.

Once spirit has disconnected from the physical, the ego, the burden, and all of life's challenges, it reconnects with Divine Source energy and all the different levels and essences that represent the Divine. Spirit comes home to love. While spirit learned countless lessons in the physical, the main lesson it remembers when it returns is that we have never been separate from God's love and have always been part of that love.

If there is any message that spirit tries to get through to us in the physical, it's that very lesson—that we are always loved and are always part of Divine energy. Often in readings, spirit tells me how much it truly loves its family, especially the recipient listening to the reading. I frequently get a feeling in my solar plexus during a session that spirit is this enormous ball of love energy that wants to radiate out to everyone possible.

Of course this isn't the only thing spirit wants to say to us when it comes through. Spirit is very chatty, and aside from giving us all the evidential information, it passes on lots of other types of messages. It may express an apology for something it did or didn't do while in the physical. Perhaps the spirit person was an abusive husband or an alcoholic while alive; now, however, they may come through with deep-felt sorrow and apologies to all the people they may have hurt either emotionally or physically. They may express a regret for a life not lived to the fullest or a regret for something they should have done while on earth.

Unlike spirit, most of us in our everyday lives here on earth go about our days thinking about what we need to do for work or what we have to do when we get home. We think about whether we need to go grocery shopping, if anyone fed the cats, or if the kids have done their homework, and on and on. We certainly are not in a mode where we contemplate how to express our love to others.

Rarely do we have time to stop and think about ourselves, let alone think about others, except perhaps family and friends. Most of our time is devoted to the endless chores we seem to have in front of us that appear to occupy more hours than exist in a day. By the time the day is done, we're exhausted and want nothing more than a good night's sleep.

Yet what did we really accomplish? Where did the day go? How did we spend our time? Were we most concerned by our own problems, or did we try to help our neighbors and those who needed help? Did we play golf, or did we feed a homeless person who had nothing to their name? Imagine if suddenly you have no concerns in the world and you could do anything you wanted. What would make you feel the best deep inside, down to your core? When presented with the following choices, which would you choose?

A) Would you go out every night and party to excess, buy expensive things, constantly travel the world, and live lavishly like an opulent king? or

B) Would you spend your time trying to help others, getting them needed food and water, putting a roof over their head, and helping them with other basic necessities?

Which set of actions shows more care for others or follows Jesus's command to "love thy neighbors as thyself"? That's easy to figure out.

We, as spirits having a human experience, know deep in our souls that love is the energy that bonds us together, now and forever. This was as true when we were little children as it is when we are in our final years on this planet. This is also true when we escape our temporary shell of a body and become part of the thriving spirit world. Nothing changes, just the vehicle containing that consciousness, which chooses to focus on love. Love is the highest energy in the universe, and like spirit and consciousness, it can never be created or destroyed; it just changes form.

Above All, That Love Is for Us

What does this have to do with spirit and its messages of love for us? A lot, actually. Spirit is much like someone who no longer has a care in the world and can do anything he wants. Spirit, of course, has no constraints. It doesn't even have an ego to weigh it down with selfish or personal concerns. As a result, most spirit people are full of love and care deeply about others. It is this wider perspective that inspires spirit to seek continued education on the other side to learn more about and grow its love. It also wants to know how love will aid its spiritual journey and help it get closer to God.

A great deal of spirit activity on earth relates to its love of mankind and its love for loved ones left behind on earth. It's often with us in an effort to express how much it loves us. While spirit is often around us, we just need to be aware of its presence, trust that it is here, and surrender to its love. It wants to help us and guide us, though due to the Law of Freewill, it isn't allowed to interfere in our lives except to alert us to its presence. Just because a person has passed into spirit doesn't mean it has lost its love for us or is not aware of us. On the contrary, now it's far more able to express its love for us than ever before and wants to let us know how much it loves us.

A Grouch in the Spirit World

Take for, example, the grumpy father who always seemed to be in a bad mood and was negative about everything and everyone around him and never had a good word to say about anybody. This describes a lot of people we know today, doesn't it? He doesn't hurt anybody; he's just an ill-tempered man who can't get along with anyone because of problems in his life. Of course he loves his children and his wife, but he is always in such a foul mood that he can never express it. He's what you might call a grouch.

Now what do you think happens when he moves on to the spirit world? Let's assume he passes from a heart attack in his fifties. Because his ego and self-centered focus have been left behind, all that's left is the realization that love conquers all. In fact, upon arrival to the afterlife, our grouch is lovingly welcomed by those who've arrived before, many of whom he knows. He is showered with love, which he accepts freely, and the joy he feels is unsurpassed by any of his earthly memories. He realizes he has entered a land of pure joy and love that emanates from everyone and everything that flows like a river without end.

His perception of existence dramatically changes for the better as he realizes he can be just as loving as all the other beings around him, for love is infectious that way. It's a pleasant change for him and something he wishes he had been able to do back while he was on earth. He realizes he should have been so much more loving to his family, his friends, his neighbors, and even people he didn't know. He deeply regrets not being more loving to people and not expressing that he did truly love them. He knows this would have made them feel so much happier at the time.

Try as he might to get his family to hear him, see him, or in some way notice him, it's to no avail. He realizes that his vibration as a spirit is so much higher than the physical human vibration that he can't be seen, heard, touched, felt, or sensed by his family. So after learning from other spirits that he could communicate with his family through a medium, he gets very excited and gets a reading setup through his family's various spirit guides. These guides train and prepare him how to communicate with the medium and give the former grouch now in spirit specific instructions that will make the session productive.

The day arrives; the evidential part of the communication goes well, and he's finally able to give his message. He expresses how sorry he is that he didn't say "I love you" enough in life. Because his personality hasn't changed, he hesitates when he mentions that he loves his family. However, with some effort, he fully expresses his total and complete love for them. He regrets the fact that he was always so foul tempered and grumpy. He also regrets that his temper ultimately had a negative effect on the children and the entire family.

This scenario is actually typical of many readings I have with families where the loved one in spirit comes through and expresses their regret that they didn't love their family enough and they want to say, now that they have the chance, how much they truly do love them.

This man's love for his family finally had a chance to come through because his perception had grown wider and lessons were learned. He had never lost his love for his family; he just had difficulty expressing it. However, in the spirit plane, he learned tremendous lessons and gained a wider understanding that helped him fully express the love that was deep inside him all along. We never lose love; it only changes form. But our loved ones in spirit are our best mentors to demonstrate that we should love everyone. They often try to remind us to love one another.

Spirit Authors

Spirit passes on its expressions of love to us both in readings and demonstrations as well as in its automatic writings. Over the last 150 years, love has been a central theme of those writings. It becomes quite clear that love is the preeminent energy in the spirit world and something spirit wants us to spread to each other. Each time I read a book written by a spirit author, I'm amazed by the insights they bring.

What's so stunning is the fact that every spirit author emphasized love's importance in the spirit world as well as in the physical. This comes through in readings and demonstrations as well. Clearly, the more we practice being loving to others in the physical, the more we grow our spirit here and in turn will more appreciate how important love is in the spirit world. The biggest takeaway I've had is that everything we do and every action we take should be centered around love and how we can help others.

While this is a beautiful and noble cause, this would initially seem to be a tall order that would be difficult for most people. Yet the missing piece I discovered was that spirit wasn't referring to huge, sacrificial actions but rather to small things that we can do every day. This spreads the feeling of love everywhere and elevates the vibration of the population one person at a time.

It's similar to the saying I've heard of "One holy moment every day." At first I thought that was impossible and required too much to accomplish. It sounded like one had to do something holy that was religious, pious, and really weighty.

In fact, it only means to do one nice thing for someone each day. Ideas that come to mind include:

- hold the door open for someone;
- help someone cross the street;
- pick up someone's newspaper for them;
- smile and be nice to someone to cheer them up;
- pay for the person behind you in a coffee line

These are tiny actions that are so easy for us that they seem almost insignificant. The thing is, though, that because we're doing something nice for a stranger out of the kindness of our heart, it is more meaningful to them, and they are more appreciative. Make someone else smile or feel good about the world and pay it forward. This becomes contagious because when others become more loving themselves, they in turn do loving things for others. Soon the entire world could be a more loving place. This is really what love is all about: doing something nice for someone else without expecting anything in return, just because it feels good. Wouldn't you love to live in a world like that? It's not difficult.

Spiritual Progression

These days, it seems more people around the world are learning to expand their spiritual awareness and consciousness. In the US, we're seeing more mind/body/spirit practitioners offering their services, meditation/yoga/Reiki are all going mainstream, topics once taboo like mediumship and spiritualism are gaining acceptance, and people are becoming more aware of their spiritual lives. People are becoming more active; they're improving their physical, emotional, and spiritual health, and they seem genuinely interested in trying to become better versions of themselves. I believe this is no accident:

spirit has been trying to spiritually awaken more people at an accelerated pace, and people are responding—whether they are doing this consciously is another question.

Yet for all the improvements in global consciousness and spiritual awareness, there remains a silent majority who continue to slumber. Entire swaths of the global population still walk the earth in a dreamlike state, as if they are sleepwalking. It appears the majority of the world still believes the physical is the reality and the nonlinear is the dream. However, spirit constantly reminds us that the reverse is in fact true. It informs us that the physical is a bad dream and the nonlinear is the awake state and more real than we could imagine, with a oneness with each other and with God. I received this while doing a trance reading in a trance development circle, and it is also written about in *A Course In Miracles* by Helen Schucman.

I've had the distinct feeling from my spirit guides that all of us who are awakening to greater realities now have the responsibility to help those who still sleepwalk to awaken and see the light—both in ourselves and in the greater truth of existence. During some recent trance mediumship development training, for example, I would begin uttering amazing comments reflecting those very thoughts.

In one instance, I stated humanity was developing and awakening at a faster rate, but there remained a huge gap that left behind a vast number of souls in the physical who had yet to awaken. I continued in that vein, pleading that it was now time for those who had awoken to raise up those still in sleep. In another case, I urged all those in the physical to deepen their love for one another, raise up one another, and help one another. The messages were clear: for any of us to progress, we need to help others progress as well. The more we help others, both physically and spiritually, the more we help ourselves. As the saying goes, "We are only as strong as our weakest link."

One theme continues to forcefully present itself as I read more spirit writing and get deeper with my spirit communication. Love is the strongest energy in existence, the power that elevates our consciousness to greater heights, and the primary link between us and the Source energy. We in the physical, who are limited in our perspective due to our ego minds, know only separation from Source and from each other. We often feel alone and separate from the rest of humanity, including from those closest to us. We feel separate from our loved ones in spirit. We feel separate from God. In short, we feel all alone and surrounded by strangers. This is part of the dream state. In fact, we are still part of the Divine, for we have the God spark inside us and are all children of God, and in turn are all related. We are all brothers and sisters in a huge, loving family connected by the common fabric of love that's interwoven in the universal tapestry. However, our spiritual amnesia prevents us from remembering where we came from and to whom we are related.

Because we are all related and part of one another, what we do to others is in fact what we are doing to ourselves. Some call this the boomerang theory, and it has unintended consequences. We may get mad that someone cuts us off in traffic and stay mad about it the rest of the day, which ruins our day and everything we try to do. The anger doesn't help anyone, not even us. It's just a downward spiral of negativity. Furthermore, that anger becomes misplaced when we realize that we are actually getting mad at ourselves, for the person who cut us off is essentially a part of us because we are all linked together. How can we fix this?

The solution lies in what spirit and others, including Jesus, have been telling us for centuries: "Love one another." Sounds like heavy stuff. Seems like something no average person on the street could possibly manage with all their everyday human stresses and problems, like mortgages, car payments, relationship issues, marital strife, bills, job insecurity, medical concerns, and on and on. Yet do you remember how good it felt when you did something nice for someone?

What goes around comes around. Some call this karma. Recall that we are all connected, and there is no separation as all is unity. Whatever you put out into the universe, you will receive back yourself. So if you want to improve how you feel and build up love and positivity for yourself, start doing loving things for others no matter how small. Furthermore, you'll get dividends for your efforts relative to the amount of positivity you invest. Due to the Law of Attraction, or "like attracts like," you'll start to get more love from the universe when you send love to others in the universe as the positive spiral moves ever upward.

In the early days of my journey, anything that contained slightly religious or even spiritual overtones made me skeptical and wary of their hidden agenda. Now, however, I've fully come to accept spirituality as not only our personal relationship with the Divine, but also how that enables us to spread love throughout the universe, each in our individual way. Nothing makes this more clear than another experience I had during one of my meditations.

In the session, I was sitting one morning by a placid lake surrounded by pine trees and snow-covered mountains. As I was taking in the scene of the lake that reflected its surroundings,

I saw an amethyst-colored line stretching along the bottom of the view. I sensed it somehow had a royal or highly spiritual meaning. Unexpectedly, I saw a tall bear with dark brown fur near me on my left. At first he was clapping his paws together, and then he hugged me in a tight embrace. He was so large that I only came up to his chest. His fur was so warm and soft that I didn't want to leave. I felt surrounded by happiness and joy like all of nature was dancing and celebrating, like I'd returned from someplace.

I saw a flash of a gravestone with a Celtic cross on it, but I began receiving an overpowering sense of unconditional love. It was so strong that it felt tangible. I was in awe and felt undeserving of this love and such an honor. The scene just stayed like this for several minutes. Then as I looked back out over the lake, I saw a large yellow light floating about ten or twenty feet above the water. Inside was an image of Christ's smiling face. I felt another warm wave of love wash over me. He told me I was loved by all, but I said I was undeserving of this honor. He calmly said that I'd been sent here to heal, comfort, and serve others. Christ also said, "Go do my mission of love and healing." Who would have thought a skeptic like me would be sent here to do work like that?!

Remember, I'm definitely not a Bible-carrying religious zealot who proclaims I've been sent by Jesus or God to do anything. I probably failed out of church school (or was never even enrolled). But that meditation sure as hell got my attention. I couldn't stop thinking about it. But what really grabbed me was that despite my protestations, fifteen minutes later while driving to work, I saw a bumper sticker on the car in front of me that read, "Jesus Loves You." When I saw that, chills ran throughout my entire body. There are no such things as coincidences.

14

A Few Readings

"At the core of any endeavor in life is your spirit self."
—Mechelle Beltran

What always amazes me is the intelligence on the other side and how spirit gets their information to us in the physical. In my readings, I receive the majority of my information through clairvoyance, clairsentience, and claircognizance. Occasionally I'll receive information through clairaudience. Getting information from spirit is like playing psychic charades, where they give me lots of images, feelings, and an awareness of something, and I have to piece everything together.

I'll give what I get, though sometimes it doesn't make any sense to me, but it has meaning to the recipient. Sometimes the communicators can be really clear and easy to understand, while other times they're difficult to perceive, just like in the real world. Remember, personalities don't change just because we lose our physical bodies.

One example of spirit's intelligence and clarity of communication can easily be seen in a reading I had with Alison, where her husband came through brilliantly. He amazed me at every turn with his crafty ways to get me to understand his ideas so I could relay them to his wife. Below is a description of her reading as well as several others (names of the recipients have been changed for the privacy of the sitters).

Alison

Alison is from the United Kingdom, so we scheduled a reading using the video chat service Skype over the internet. Not only could we see and hear each other, but the connection was free, definitely a plus. Since distance is a physical and human construct, it made no difference to spirit where we were physically located so long as we could generate enough energy to attract spirit to us. What I found notable about this session was the great imagery and use of numerous symbols. It was a clairvoyant's ideal reading.

Alison and I exchanged pleasantries, after which I went through my usual explanation of how I work, and then I said a prayer to open the energy. Soon I saw in my mind's eye a man greater than six feet tall, with big hands, thick fingers, broad shoulders, a large chest, but a narrow waist. I could tell by his large arm muscles that he could easily lift heavy objects, and I thought he must be showing me himself in his prime. As I ran my hand along my imaginary timeline, an unseen force compelled me to stop in the sixties age bracket. I relayed everything I saw and felt.

"Alison, does the description of this man make sense to you?"

"Yes. I knew a man just like him."

"And the age of his passing also makes sense to you?"

"Yes."

As the man placed both hands on the center of his chest, I quickly felt pain in the center of my chest, which made me think initially that he had passed from a heart attack. However, my breathing subsequently became labored and difficult as each inhalation grew shallower. Thoughts of cigarettes and smoking dropped into my head, which together with the breathing problems and chest pains made me think this man had lung problems. I described what the man had shown me and let me feel.

"I feel like this man passed from an issue related to his lungs."

"No, he didn't pass from a lung problem. He had a heart attack."

Had I stayed with my first impression, a heart attack, I would have been accurate on the first try. I learned my lesson again: Always go with your first instinct, trust what you receive, and give what you get rather than interpret. Maybe the cigarettes just contributed to his heart condition, though the clue threw me off. Regardless, I had allowed my conscious mind to interfere.

I invited this man's spirit to draw closer to me so we could blend our energies. I always give spirit permission to blend and merge its soul with mine so that I can truly feel who they are and step into their shoes. This way I can better paint them back to life for the sitter. When I get a strong link with spirit they will often overshadow me, and I'll take on their mannerisms, ways of speaking, and gestures. As I allowed this man to overshadow me, my heart expanded with immense compassion, caring, and selfless love, which helped me understand his character. He added greater color and dimension to the portrait he was painting of himself by dropping the words and phrases "warm," "tender" and "wouldn't hurt a fly" into my mind. I passed on all of this information.

"Alison, do these descriptions match this same man we've been discussing?"

"Yes."

"I'm also being made aware of a special bond, a family bond of someone very close, like a husband. I feel like this is your husband. Would you understand that to be true?"

"Yes."

After a brief pause, the man showed me an image of an ax, followed by a trowel and a garden, which by themselves meant nothing. However, I began to think they were all symbols for outdoor activities and gardening. As I realized this, a desire to go outdoors, interact with nature and get my hands dirty tending to flowers overwhelmed me. The picture began to come together and was quite clear.

"He's now showing me himself gardening and also getting close to nature. I sense this man's interests and hobbies lay in gardening and relaxing outdoors. Would you understand this?"

"Yes, he spent hours tending to his lovely flowers in that garden."

"Alison, I just heard the phrase, 'tea and biscuits.' I don't know what this phrase means. Does this make any sense to you?"

"Well, I know many people here in the UK like sitting for tea and biscuits in the afternoon, but my husband liked coffee more than tea, so no, I can't understand it either."

I couldn't figure out why her husband was showing me tea

and biscuits, so I asked her husband to explain what he meant and why he was showing me this. Nothing. Then I asked him to show me something that would resonate with Alison. I began to see a picture of a thick white sweater that buttoned up the middle with wooden buttons and had a wide collar. I thought it looked like a cardigan.

"Would this image of a cardigan have any significance or meaning for you?"

"No, he didn't have a sweater like that."

However, her husband wasn't giving up yet—he let me know the tea and biscuits and the sweater were both symbols for comfort. He also showed himself during the wintertime, bundled in his cardigan and sitting in his armchair at a 45-degree angle to the fireplace. His legs were wrapped in a blanket with his feet stretched out toward the hearth. I couldn't see any lights nearby, and felt he liked to keep the lights off so he could be surrounded by the orange glow of the fireplace. The warmth of the fire combined with the coziness of the sweater enabled me to melt into the plush cushions of the armchair in which I sat; I smiled with content.

"I feel this fireplace had a great deal of meaning for your husband and was a great memory for him."

"Oh, it was, yes. He adored that fireplace and sat there all winter."

"He's now showing me himself wearing warm fluffy slippers. However, I'm getting the sense they're more symbols. I feel he liked to wear warm, fluffy, soft, comfortable clothes, perhaps like that cardigan he presented to me previously. Would you understand this?"

"Ah, yes, now I see. That's right."

"Your husband is now showing me a glass object hanging

from a gold necklace that I feel has significance for you. Do you understand the significance behind a glass object on a gold necklace?"

"No, I can't place it. It doesn't resonate."

However, again her husband wanted to get his point across and wouldn't let this go. It was clear this was an important object, so I tried to figure it out and get more clarity. As I looked closer at the glass object, I thought it was a crafted glass sphere or gem, clearly something significant. Alison still couldn't place it, but her husband was quite persistent with the image. Hard as I tried, I couldn't understand what her husband was showing me, nor could I get Alison to understand it. Consequently, I left Alison with the image for her to think about later. Perhaps she might recognize the item at some later date.

After I asked for additional significant items, her husband showed me a bat and a baseball in succession. An urge welled up inside me to begin talking about them emphatically, and I sensed they were important to Alison's husband. However, Alison couldn't understand the image. I started to think this might be symbolic, which forced me to interpret its meaning—something I don't like to do. Since Alison and her husband were from the UK, I thought it might be significant for someone British, so I considered the British equivalent to baseball, which was cricket. I thus presumed her husband liked cricket.

"Alison, I'm sensing these are symbols for cricket. I take it your husband liked cricket?"

"Yes, that's correct. He did like cricket. He played the game here in the UK. He was on one of our big teams over here."

I sat there amazed at spirit's ingenuity to help me arrive at this conclusion.

I asked Alison's husband to give me anything that would help me describe him better and paint him back to life. No sooner had I thought that than I immediately pictured a large family and wanted to throw out my arms and my love to everyone around me. My chest and heart began to expand, my shoulders seemed to widen, my arm muscles flexed, and I thought I grew six inches. I became the family patriarch and protector of a big family with tremendous amounts of love that emanated from every pore.

"Alison, does this feeling of a loving, protective family man make sense to you?"

"Oh, yes, absolutely. He was quite a family man."

Unfortunately, this feeling of a loving protector didn't last long. Soon I envisioned myself as a child, and my heart ached from terrible solitude and loneliness mixed with a profound lack of love. I became aware that when this man had a family of his own, he overcompensated for his childhood experiences and made everyone feel loved and part of the family. I felt a sharp contrast between his small, lonely childhood and his warm, loving, tight-knit family as an adult. Alison heartily agreed with this description.

Alison's husband subsequently showed me a four poster bed, but that didn't resonate with her. It was clearly another symbol, however, as it brought my attention to a bed. Then the man showed me the same bed at nighttime, at which point subtle pains shot through my chest.

"I feel like your husband had his heart attack at night while in bed. Does this make sense to you?"

"Yes."

Next, I saw an image of a peanut butter jar, and I got the

feeling that I get when I eat peanut butter too fast. When I do that, it sometimes gives me a pain in my chest because it gets clogged up in my esophagus. I feel like I'm having angina, or perhaps a precursor to a heart attack, but I'm never quite sure what I should do about the feeling in my chest.

As I was seeing the peanut butter jar, I recalled that painful feeling I get in my chest when I eat peanut butter too fast. In the same way, I sensed Alison's husband wasn't sure what to do about his chest pains, so he went to the hospital that night, where he had another heart attack and passed. Alison confirmed this.

Then her husband started sending his messages for me to relay. At first, a sense of peace and calm washed over me from outside of me, which let me know this was his existence. I became aware he could see everything clearly and from a different perspective, while he had learned to substantially expand his love in the nonphysical realm. He spread his arms wide as he sent his love to everyone he'd ever known, and it was to a greater degree than he could have shared while alive on earth.

He then showed me a watering can, which by itself it meant nothing to me. However, he then added an image of himself up in the clouds showering Alison with love from that watering can. This reminded me of the earlier image of him relaxing in his garden. He started puckering his lips and blowing Alison lots of kisses. I described this for her.

"Does this make sense to you? Does that fit your husband's personality?"

Alison choked back tears as she responded, "Oh, lordy. Yes, this was something he often did while he was alive."

"I sense your husband was unusually tender and affectionate.

He's making me aware that he liked to stroke your shoulder often. He's also making me aware that recently he's alerted you to his presence by stroking your right shoulder as he stood behind you. You might have felt this as an unexplained energy. Would you recognize that?"

"Yes, he often used to stroke my shoulders when he was here. Funny you should say that because recently I have felt some strange, tingling energies around me, especially on my shoulders. Wow, was that really him?"

I then heard Alison's husband begin to speak, and I relayed his words.

"I want to let you know that I'm still here. I'm with you all the time, and I feel your feelings and hear your thoughts. I still love you, Alison, and I just can't wait until we're together again."

Her husband continued on, helping Alison recall their tremendous bond, affection, endearment, and strong love that kept them together and always would. I felt that her husband hadn't been gone terribly long, but his ability to communicate was very impressive and quite accurate. He did a fantastic job coming through and letting Alison know he was still quite alive and that he loved her tremendously.

Celia

Perhaps the best example of spirit demonstrating that they still remember us and are watching over us comes from a reading I did for Celia. When I first went to Celia's house, I wasn't sure what to expect, but I was pleasantly surprised to find a warm, smiling face on the person who greeted me at the door. We chatted for a while, and I began to describe what I do and how the session would work. I described the concept of the three-way energy cocktail and the need for positivity in the room, and encouraged her to be open for anything that might happen. She agreed, and I got underway.

I soon noticed spirit's call sign and signal that it was ready to help me: I began to feel tingling around my shoulders. My heart beat increased, my energy levels grew, and my breathing became fast and shallow, three indications that spirit was close at hand. I got up from my chair, began to pace and rub my hands together vigorously as the energy continued to build. I couldn't relax. Mind you, these are all good signs because spirit's vibrations are very high compared to our dense and low vibrations, so it's no wonder I was feeling jittery and high strung.

I sensed a tall man by my side who had strong, clean hands. As he drew closer to me and started to overshadow me, I sensed the man had a strong, gruff personality, yet was quiet and didn't seem quite sure of what he wanted to do. He had difficulty expressing his emotions and just stood there beside me with a blank expression. The man wore a suit, looking like he worked in an office, and gave the appearance he was fairly successful. His clothes were dark, and in some odd way the man seemed to match the clothes. I described everything I felt and saw.

"Celia, I'm beginning to get the feeling this is your father. Does all of this make sense to you?"

"Yes, that sounds quite accurate."

"I'm getting a slight pain in my chest. I feel that your father passed from a condition related to the chest area, perhaps a failing heart or a heart attack. Would you understand that?"

"You're right, he did have a heart attack."

I ran my hands along an imaginary timeline from left to right, but as I neared the seventies and eighties age brackets, I felt like I couldn't or didn't want to move past there. I suggested to Celia that it felt like her father passed in his seventies or eighties because I couldn't get past that time frame. She said she understood what I was saying, as her father passed away when he was eighty-two. Then her father seemed to step back and allow someone else to begin communicating with me.

The energy near me increased rather abruptly, and I felt like I just wanted to dance and sing and party. Against the dark, empty background in my mind, I began to see an image of a woman with fine features, and I sensed she had a strong personality and immense compassion. Her hair was dark brown with a red tint. She felt like a tender, loving mother. She had an incredibly gregarious and fun-loving personality, and she seemed like she was person who loved being the center of attention at a party. When I did her timeline, I wanted to stop in the sixties or seventies. I detailed everything I saw and felt.

"Celia, I'm sure your mother is stepping forward now. She's quite gregarious and fun loving. I feel like she passed in her sixties or seventies. Does that make sense to you?"

"I can take everything you said. In fact, she died at age sixty-five."

Her mother had a beautiful face with a wide smile and gave me the impression she was so happy to be reuniting with her daughter again. She exuded a warm and loving energy, yet I simultaneously felt that she wouldn't tolerate people stepping out of line.

The closer she blended with me, the more I used phrases and sayings Celia's mother had used. I also began waving my hands and arms and making specific gestures and mannerisms.

"That's what my mother used to do!" Celia yelled with excitement.

Then her mother started to make motions I couldn't understand at first. I saw her kneeling at the feet of two small children and stroking their hair, and I felt these were Celia's two daughters. Then she stood up, and I began to get the feeling of greater height and growth, as if to acknowledge they had grown up.

"Celia, your mother just stood up after kneeling at the feet of two small children. Does this make any sense to you?"

As tears began to slowly stream down her face, Celia nodded vigorously, and a warm smile of recognition appeared. Celia's mother effortlessly floated to her and threw her arms around Celia's shoulders, while her father approached and just began to pat her head, but soon he too came in for a hug.

Then the messages began. The mother, being the more outgoing one, started first.

"Your mother is letting me know she's so proud of you for raising two daughters on your own, after your nasty divorce. She's mentioning to me that she's watched the girls grow up and couldn't be happier about how they turned out. She loves you tremendously and has been helping you from the other side."

Celia nodded her head and wiped the tears from her face.

"Your father is expressing regret at not being with you enough when you were a child. He's sorry he wasn't able to stay on the earth long enough to be with you. He's just pointing to you and letting me feel his love for you."

I paused to let Celia digest these messages, and we closed the reading with a prayer.

"Chris, thank you so much connecting me with my parents.

Hearing from them was quite meaningful, and it felt so good to be in touch with them again. It also helped me to understand my mother's relationship with my children, whom she never met because she passed on before they were born. Getting my parents' loving messages gave me a feeling of inner wellness."

This is another example of why I love being a medium. The transformational love from spirit has such healing power for the recipient that it overwhelms me. Since I'm the instrument delivering the messages containing loving healing, I wind up getting a residual healing. I love seeing the reunions and the healings, and I love being healed myself.

Emily

Emily and her husband came to see me one afternoon in an effort to reconnect with her brother. This was quite a different reading than normal, because when Emily and her husband arrived, I wasn't mentally prepared for the appointment because I had lost track of time. Consequently, I was a bit flustered when they showed up at my door. I escorted them to my living room to let them wait briefly as I went upstairs to prepare and get ready.

When I came back downstairs, I suggested we sit down at the dining room table where we might be able to work more effectively. As I began to go through my preamble and typical opening statements, I stretched out my right arm toward an empty dining room chair to my right. To my surprise, it felt like I'd put my arm through a tingling auric energy field belonging to someone sitting in the chair! No doubt, spirit had already arrived.

My mind was still in a frenzied, hyperactive, chaotic state

after Emily appeared. Thinking about this in retrospect, perhaps this was a good thing because it kept my mind in a high vibrational state, perfect for communicating with spirit. The one drawback was that I couldn't focus or clear my mind. Normally, I try to calm myself and imagine looking into a dark, empty room or envision spirit placing its hand on my right shoulder. However, in my current frame of mind, I couldn't do either.

In desperation, I tried a different tactic. Medium Tony Stockwell once taught me a wonderful exercise for improving my focus during readings and meditation. He suggested I focus on a candle flame, as that would enable me to remove distractions and allow my mind to become a clear, empty screen ready for spirit to work. At this point I couldn't think of any other alternatives, so I tried his suggestion and hoped for the best.

I began to envision in my mind a bright white flame burning atop a candle. I could see the bulbous base of the flame, the graceful curves of the flame narrowing up to the tip, the occasional flicker of the flame, and a faint, light-yellow glow emanating from the flame itself, almost like an aura. Within seconds, this vision wiped my mind clear of all thoughts and, just like Tony suggested, offered a blank canvas upon which spirit could paint.

No sooner had I focused on this candle flame than in my mind's eye a young man in front of me began jumping up and down, waving his arms at me in a frantic attempt to catch my attention. He presented himself in his late teens or early twenties, wearing a plaid flannel shirt and jeans with a rip on the left knee. I could see, hiding underneath an emotionless face, a smile was hiding that was trying to come out. Consequently, I felt he showed most people a slightly reserved personality, yet he let his more mischievous and spunky side come out to his close friends.

"Emily, do you recognize this young man?"

"Yes, you perfectly described my brother."

Soon Emily's brother gave me an image of himself standing on a black lava flow as large as a boulder against a sunny blue sky. Off to my left I saw lush, dark-green grass on a hill gently sloping up and away to the left. To my right I saw a cliff with the ocean below and water crashing against the beach into a foamy residue. In front of the black lava mass and crossing diagonally in front of me up to my left, I saw a dirt road or path that extended far into the distance.

"Does this scene hold any significance for you?"

"Yes. That was on our vacation," Emily and her husband both said.

Her brother provided additional pieces of evidence, but one in particular hit home. I asked him to give me significant information that would have real meaning for Emily. Suddenly, I saw a bright, white hospital corridor with a young man on an emergency room stretcher that had its metal sides raised up. I could see the gurney as if I was standing at the patient's feet pushing it forward. Hospital staff grasped the stretcher's side rails on either side and thrust it forward like there was no time to waste. They pushed it so fast that the gurney crashed through a set of swinging double doors into another hall, like this was a life-and-death situation with only seconds remaining, and they were doing everything they could to save his life.

"Do you understand this scene and who's on the stretcher?"

Emily was so emotional by this point that all she could do

was nod her head and use her trembling hand to wipe away the tears that were streaming down her face.

Suddenly, an unseen force gripped my entire body and prevented it from moving, while simultaneously an electric energy ran from my head to my toes. My arms and hands started to quiver and shake, almost like I was having convulsions or a seizure. An intense pressure began squeezing my head and brain like a huge vice, while I thought my brain was getting ready to explode. I described what I was feeling, and Emily again nodded her head, but her sobbing only intensified.

After providing unique and emotional evidence that left no doubt he was present, Emily's brother offered additional, less-upsetting evidence for his sister. The scenery before me changed to an evening luau. I could see a rectangular patio with a large ceremonial fire at the center, complete with tiki torches and lush vegetation all around. Off to my right in the distance, I could hear the intense and frenzied beating of ceremonial Hawaiian drums. A large, open-air Polynesian-style building with a thatched roof stood off to my left. A group of five or six people stood in the hut watching the ceremony, but I felt they all knew each other and came here to celebrate something.

"I just heard the phrase 'sweet sixteen,' but that doesn't make any sense to me. I usually associate that phrase with a girl's birthday party. Maybe it's symbolic for someone's birthday, or perhaps the number sixteen is significant. Would either of those make any sense to you?"

"No, I don't see how that connects." Emily sniffled.

"Maybe the phrase represents a party bringing together many people your brother knew. Perhaps it relates to the image I received about the people standing in the hut."

"That makes sense. The luau was a family party, and everyone there knew each other."

"Four of the five people in the hut were also in the hospital waiting area when Emily's brother was rushed to the emergency room," her husband said.

After a brief pause without any information, Emily's brother brought me to a bright, white, empty space with a foggy background where I could see him calmly standing before me. I sensed he was trying to show me his representation of the spirit world. Unexpectedly he began dancing what looked like an Irish jig; he leapt high in the air and clicked his heels together repeatedly. A broad smile crossed his face, and his arms stretched up and out to his sides as he continued to dance, exuding happiness, joy, and freedom. After jumping up, he continued to fly through the air like Peter Pan, free as a bird. I realized Emily's brother was relaying how happy and free he now felt in the spirit world, and that any pain and limitation he previously had in the physical world had disappeared. My heart began to swell like a balloon.

"Your brother is showing me himself in the spirit world, smiling and dancing. He's flying around free as a bird, with no physical limitations, and appears quite happy."

Emily appeared visibly relieved as a faint smile crossed her face.

"I'm hearing 'I'm sorry' and 'I'm sorry I didn't do more.' Would you understand that? Does that make sense?"

Emily nodded, but tears began to fall again.

"I regret not taking care of myself. I'm responsible, so don't blame yourself. You did everything you could have done." Emily just wiped the tears from her face and nodded.

"I love ya, sis," her brother said as he began to wave at her.

He turned around and started to walk away along a path that curved up to my right. As he followed the path with his back to me, he put his right hand over his left shoulder and started waving at his sister. Then he slowly disappeared in a bank of fuzzy white clouds. Emily sat silently in her chair for a few moments and looked down at the table with an empty gaze.

Her husband broke the silence and asked, "What can I do to help Emily?"

Before Emily's husband had even finished his question, her brother was already saying, "You're a stand-up guy. Just keep doing what you're doing. Support her and stand by her side." Her husband turned to look at Emily, put his right hand gently on her left shoulder, and nodded as he softly bit his lip.

At the end of the reading, I just sat quietly in my chair and allowed both Emily and her husband to slowly absorb everything they'd heard. They had a lot to process and needed time to gather their thoughts. Emily's brother had given her a beautiful and transformational healing based on love. He was still with her and watching over her. I could tell she now understood this because she looked like she'd experienced an epiphany or received some revelation and knowledge, unlike when she was standing at my door and wore an expression of uncertainty.

"This was incredible. Thank you so much," Emily's husband said.

"No, thank Emily's brother," I responded. "He did all the work."

I had to admit I felt healed myself. Spirit's transformative love graced us all that day and brought healing where it was needed.

Lydia

Lydia was from England and booked an appointment with me for a reading over Skype in an effort to hear from her family members in spirit. I found her session quite moving. At first I connected with a woman who emanated nurturing, comforting, caring, and loving vibrations like a motherly figure. However, I sensed she came from a similar generation as Lydia's mother, but connected to her mother's side of the family. As I ran my hand over my imaginary timeline, I couldn't get past the sixty age bracket; my indication that she passed in her sixties. I began to see the woman's image change from quite skinny to quite overweight suddenly as a slight pain grew in my midsection. I felt she passed of a stomach-related disease that caused her to quickly gain weight. I described what I had seen and felt.

"Lydia, do you recognize this woman?"

"Yes. That's my aunt."

"She's showing me around her house now. It's absolutely spotless, and everything appears neatly organized. I sense she was quite fastidious and cleaned her house several times per week. I feel this woman was a housewife who was very house proud. Would you understand this about her?"

"Yes. She used to clean her house *every day*, not just a few times a week."

Lydia's aunt began to give me a remarkably detailed 360-degree remote viewing of what her house used to look like, especially her living room. To my right I saw a love seat with bright yellow upholstery in front of matching floor-to-ceiling drapes on either side of a window that overlooked a beautiful garden. In front of the love seat sat a coffee table that was neatly stacked with magazines, and a colorful oval rug lay in front of a brick fireplace off to my left, centered on the front wall of the living room. A tremendous amount of sunshine streamed in through the tall windows making the room feel spacious and bright.

As I looked more closely at her bright face, I saw this woman kept a happy disposition and a broad smile, even when things in her life got her down. She'd never let others know that she was depressed, as she would always put on a happy face in public. At one point I could see a weak smile on her face, but her eyes revealed a sadness that belied a strain and true unhappiness underneath her exterior. Then she began to impress upon me thoughts using clairaudience.

At first I heard the refrain from the song "Come On Eileen" by Dexy's Midnight Runners, which was a song I recalled from my high school years describing a woman named Eileen. I didn't know what it meant or its significance, so I just told Lydia what I heard.

"Does this phrase or the name Eileen mean anything to you at all?"

"Sure. It's certainly a reference to a close relative of mine named Eileen. I was thinking about her just the other day."

"Now I'm hearing 'She minds her Ps and Qs.' Would you understand this?"

"Well, in the UK, people say that when they're describing someone who doesn't swear, speaks politely, and is quite formal. I'd say that phrase perfectly fits the woman you've got."

Then Lydia's aunt stepped back slightly and brought in a tall man who was well over six feet tall. His expressionless face, narrow eyes, and furrowed brow suggested a cold personality.

I sensed he had become distant, aloof, and no longer connected with the woman who stood near him. He wore a handlebar mustache, and a pipe rested in the right corner of his mouth. This man also wore a flat, tweed driver's cap, dirty boots, scruffy pants, and a tweed jacket over a dark work shirt, as if he lived in the countryside rather than an urban area. I described this new contact.

"Oh, yes. This fella's my aunt's first ex-husband. Nasty divorce."

He looked down at Lydia's aunt as she looked up at him. Suddenly a smile broke across his face as his personality began to lighten and his warmth shined through. As their arms intertwined, I could see they enjoyed standing together again as love melted the previously icy relationship. Lydia thanked me for letting her know they were together again in the spirit world surrounded by love, and that they were still in her life.

Mitch

As Mitch and I sat down and exchanged pleasantries, he squirmed in his chair. While I described the spirit communication process, he glared at me with furrowed brow and pursed lips that belied his skepticism. The grunts and guttural sounds that emerged from his mouth, together with his quizzical expression, built a wall of nonresponse around him that would be difficult to penetrate. He clearly wasn't overly enthused about the reading, and I wasn't sure why he'd even decided to make an appointment. I didn't detect much interest from either his comments or the tone of his voice, let alone a sense of happiness or excitement in his life. Despite the negativity and disbelief that pervaded the room, I progressed with the reading. Since spirit often orchestrates how readings come together, and they had likely brought Mitch to me for this session, I felt it was my responsibility to continue.

As I connected with spirit and focused on the dark, empty movie screen in my mind, a man drew near from my right who presented himself as middle-aged, around his late fifties or early sixties. His large arms swung loosely by his side, while his protruding belly jiggled as he walked. When I looked at his face, jowls sagged around a frowning mouth, wrinkles covered his forehead, and eyelids drooped like a basset hound. I asked him what he liked to do for fun, but I just heard deafening silence. To me that shouted he never had fun when he was alive, nor was he a very communicative person.

"Mitch, would you recognize this person?"

"Yeah," he grunted.

Mitch sounded as excited about life as this man did. As that thought crossed my mind, I became aware of a family bond and kinship, suggesting to me that this man was related to Mitch, but more laterally, the way a brother might be. However, I started getting conflicting feelings as I sensed that he was not terribly close to Mitch, making me think at first that he wasn't a relative, but perhaps a friend. Given the similarity between the two men at this point in the reading, I still thought this man might be a brother, but perhaps circumstances had caused him to be distant.

As this brother figure overshadowed me, I wanted to become more disagreeable and argumentative, avoid people, and wear an invisible shell to protect myself from the world. However, I yearned for the companionship of other people and despised the loneliness that pervaded my being on the inside as a result of erecting external barriers. Again, I asked Mitch if he recognized this man.

"Uh-huh."

"Mitch, this man feels like a brother, but he also feels distant for some reason. Does that make any sense to you?"

"Yep. That sounds like my brother. He was twelve years older than I was, so we never had anything in common. Our relationship was kinda distant, and we didn't get along too well."

As I continued my description, I continued discussing the man's chest and how that was part of his defense and image to the outside world. Soon I noticed that my hand kept coming back to the center of my chest, and I was always pointing to the middle of it. The more I kept pointing at the center of my chest, the more I noticed a subtle discomfort there that kept growing. I realized that Mitch's brother was letting me know he had a health problem localized in the center of the chest, where the heart is.

"Mitch, because I keep getting these pangs in my chest and your brother keeps me pointing to the middle of my chest, I gathered he passed from a heart condition, like a heart attack. Can you take that?"

"Yeah, he died from some problem with his heart."

Mitch's brother offered a shared memory about the two brothers in a quiet, dimly lit bar. In front of me I saw a long bar with the two of them sitting side by side on the last two stools on the left-hand side. No one else sat near them, giving them relative privacy for a conversation. Both brothers slightly leaned in and intently stared at each other, engrossed in a serious, heartfelt conversation. The older one rested his hand on Mitch's shoulder as if he were giving him some form of counsel. The establishment was fairly long and stretched for some distance off to my right. Only low murmurs echoed through the bar from the few patrons there as no music played. I relayed this to Mitch.

"Oh, yeah. I remember that. It was so unusual 'cause it was like two brothers finally bonding and sharing their feelings with each other. We *never* did that, 'cept that one time."

Soon the scene changed to a small room with a window on the wall diagonally to my left, under which lay a bed with a single mattress. A tall middle-aged man stood with his back to me, staring at the bed like he was thinking about getting into it. An ephemeral image similar to Mitch's brother passed me and approached Mitch from behind, poking him in the back. When Mitch turned around, no one was there. This scenario replayed in several different places, with the result always the same as Mitch turned around without seeing anyone in sight.

"Mitch, I keep seeing an image that looks like your brother poking you from behind several times. However, each time you turn around, no one's there. Would you understand this?"

Suddenly, Mitch's eyes opened wide, his jaw dropped, and a look of bewilderment mixed with amazement crossed his face while he inhaled quickly.

"Oh my God! I felt someone poke me in my back around my house at least five times. I couldn't figure it out 'cause I live alone. It got kinda creepy, since every time I turned around, no one was there. Ya mean that entire time it was my brother?"

Mitch's brother began giving messages. I heard that he regretted not living his life to the fullest and not traveling more. I saw him holding a beach ball, which is often a symbol representing the need for a person to have more fun. He pushed it toward Mitch, suggesting that Mitch needed to have more fun, something I silently agreed with. I then saw him in the prime of his life, in full health and quite trim. He was dancing, almost frolicking, in the spirit world, showing that he was now having the time of his life, quite a contrast with his experiences on earth.

I passed these messages on to Mitch, whose tone sounded lighter and less weighed down with the burdens of life. His brother had finally gotten through to him from the other side and convinced him that not only did life continue, but that he remained with Mitch. Despite the less-than-positive atmosphere at the beginning, the reading demonstrated how spirit watches over us, can tell what's happening in our lives, and encourages us to do our best to improve our lives. Witnessing Mitch's transformation from skeptic to believer was priceless and made me feel how strong spirit's love really is.

Taylor

I was privileged to have the beautiful experience of bringing together a woman and her deceased mother for a moving and transformative spirit communication. The reading brought through truly amazing evidence that surprised me as much as the sitter. It was a clear example of how real and loving spirit truly is. It further showed me and the sitter, Taylor, that spirit absolutely knows what we need and guides us toward it. I brought through her adoptive mother who was quite expressive and specific, and a wonderful communicator.

As I started my reading for Taylor, I could hear the skepticism and hesitation in her voice. Initially she didn't seem overly enthused, although I did sense she was at least open to the process. However, she let me know right upfront about her previous bad experiences.

"I'll tell you now, most of the mediums I've seen before weren't able to connect with my spirits and family members on the other side. I felt most of them were unscrupulous or phony. For example, I once went to a supposedly 'great' medium who was very expensive, but she didn't pick up a thing for me or my friend."

I knew this reading would be no walk in the park. This made me determined to help spirit prove itself. As I tried to connect with spirit initially, I couldn't see or feel anyone near me, which made me worry the reading might not work. I relaxed and invited spirit to draw closer as I focused on my breathing. Soon a tall, animated woman practically bounced into view in my empty, dark room within my mind. She moved about briskly, and her stern eyes revealed a determination to maintain order. Her hair fell carelessly to her shoulders, as if her appearance were the last thing on her mind, and the skin on her face appeared weathered and worn. I felt this woman was experiencing some kind of struggle or tug-of-war that drained her as she spent most of her energy dealing with other people.

"Taylor," I explained, "a tall, animated woman is standing on my right. She has quite intense, energetic eyes, she moves about quickly, and her hair appears slightly disheveled. Her face seems aged from stress. Her high energy levels feel notable, especially since they appear to be directed to others. She feels like a mother figure to me and is quite close to you. However, I sense there's something separating you two. Would you recognize this person?"

"Yes. The separation might be a reference to the fact that I was adopted."

As Taylor's mother leaned in closer to me, the vibrations and tingling sensations around my arms grew more intense. I encouraged her to overshadow me, which enabled me to take on parts of her personality. Soon, a compulsion within me grew to control my family and my home. I wanted to domineer those around me, especially Taylor.

I started to see an image of a long stable with horses in it. One trainer entered from the far end, struggling to get one reluctant horse or bucking bronco into its stable. I sensed Taylor's mother was showing me a symbolic reference that raising Taylor had been similar to corralling a bucking bronco. I described everything I'd just seen.

Taylor burst out laughing. "Oh my God! That's unbelievable. It's crazy. It totally describes my relationship with my mom to a T. That really hits home 'cause I was a fiery spirit when I was younger. Let me tell you, I nearly fell off my chair just now."

"So is it safe to assume that makes sense to you?"

"Damn right. What you said was really significant because she always made reference to how she felt she had to 'corral' me into something like a barn. The horse fits my sign too."

I asked her mother for more evidence. Soon she began to provide me with some wonderful remote viewing. I saw her comfortably sitting in a soft recliner at a 45-degree angle to a fireplace, reading a book. Her feet rested on an ottoman, with legs wrapped by a gray-and-red plaid wool blanket. She held a hardcover book in her hands and kept bringing my attention back to this book, suggesting it was quite important to her. As I looked closer at it, I could see many important pieces of paper had been placed in it, but I couldn't tell what the book was.

"Taylor, would you understand this scene your mother's giving me?"

"Oh, sure. That's our living room. Mom loved sitting in front of that fireplace. The book you described was a family Bible. She was always reading that."

The scene panned over to my left. I saw a love seat with rough brown fabric in front of the left wall of the living room, and to the left of the love seat was a series of doorways to two other rooms. I traveled to the farthest room first. Against the most distant but shorter wall stood a refrigerator. On the longer wall, slightly to my right, I saw a row of cabinets and a tall window, below which stood a sink and a long counter. As I stepped back into a room between the kitchen and living room, I became aware of a little room with a small window in it and a rectangular metal dining table. I let Taylor know what I saw.

"That's a good description of the first floor layout in my mom's house. You got the living room, the little dining room, and the kitchen beyond it. That makes sense."

Soon, I began to see a scene unfold in my mind that looked like some party being held in her mother's living room. I saw a large group of people standing together who knew each other quite well, all with smiles on their faces, laughing and having a good time. I saw in the back left corner of the room a tall pine tree that was partially decorated with Christmas ornaments; a bowl of eggnog sat next to the tree. This seemed to be a festive occasion, complete with family members putting ornaments on the tree. I felt this was a regular tradition and a big affair, with lots of celebrating.

"Taylor, your mom's showing me a shared memory of

you and your family in your mother's living room at a tree trimming party. Everyone's having a great time, especially with the eggnog. It looks like a annual event. Does this make sense to you?"

"Yeah. Those were great times when our entire family got together. The eggnog helped everyone bury the hatchet, and we all got along so well then. Those were happy moments."

I looked at Taylor. She sat in her chair looking off into the distance with a smile on her face. Her mind was drifting back to happier times. The previously skeptical, no-nonsense woman now looked like she'd been touched deep inside. What I found so special about Taylor's reading was the transformational impact it had on her. It brought together both Taylor and her mother and helped validate for Taylor that her mother is still with her and loves her. It also brought her a sense of peace, happiness, and hope. This is why I'm a medium.

Later Taylor called me up to thank me for the reading. I asked her a few questions about our session.

"Taylor, what was your prior exposure to spirit before the session?"

"I always had a strong connection to spirit through spirituality. However, I hadn't met many mediums I was able to work with or who were able to read me. I couldn't really find any mediums who could connect with me."

"How did you feel before the reading began? When we started you seemed pretty skeptical."

"Despite my prior skepticism, I was open to the reading because I just felt it was going to go well. I looked at your face, and I seemed to be drawn by your energy. For some reason I felt 'safe.' I went in with an open mind and thought you were full of peace and compassion. I sensed a connection with you, which I found interesting since I typically don't trust many people."

"How did you feel as your mother's spirit was making itself known to you?"

"I was happy and excited because I'd finally met someone who was able to connect to my family in spirit. You got great information that was very specific about my mom that you could never have known. Once that began, it was obvious she began to open up more and more to you with additional information. My relatives usually don't come through to people they don't trust."

"How did you know what spirits were coming through and that they're real?"

"You were giving me specific information about my mom. For example, you described my mom sitting in her recliner in front of the fireplace at an angle reading a book, but everything was in detail and specific. You also began to talk about her Bible and everything that was in it and how important it was. There was no way you could have been that specific if it hadn't been real, if my mom hadn't been talking to you. No one knew that stuff."

"How did your feelings change over the course of the reading?"

"I really felt more peaceful and in touch with my mom's spirit. I really felt her energy and her white light come over me. I kept my arms and legs uncrossed so I could remain open. I began to feel more hopeful and more happy. I got validation to progress in my life and that I'm on the right path, which gave me hope."

"How would you compare your views of mediumship before

and after the reading?"

"The reading validated for me that others *can* connect with the other side for real. Now I feel that mediumship is given to those people who are real and genuine on the inside."

"What do you think you've learned or taken away from the reading?"

"It helped me be able to believe in mediumship more. Now I feel happier. I'm able to believe also that there are good people in the world, and now I'm opening up to others again. This reading brought more trust, and it increased my hope about people. I'm happier for the experience, and now I'm able to even progress with my book!"

Mary

The reading I gave Mary was a beautiful example of a loving communication from a devoted husband in spirit to his wife on earth who missed him dearly. I arrived at Mary's house during the snowy holiday season to find all her festive ornaments displayed with care around the house, both inside and outside. As I stood at the door waiting for Mary to let me in, I noticed a holiday sign on the door that read Believe. I immediately recognized a deeper meaning beyond the faith in Santa Claus and the Christmas miracle, but also as a belief in everlasting life.

Mary greeted me at the door and cheerfully welcomed me into her house. I didn't have a clue she had just lost her husband only eighteen months prior, for she seemed the personification of happiness. As I walked inside, I noticed a number of atypical holiday ornaments, especially many red cardinals of all shapes, sizes, and configurations placed throughout the house. Something began telling me red cardinals were significant in Mary's life, but I'd only find out exactly how significant later during my reading.

As I began, I was sitting with Mary at her rectangular dining table. I quickly felt and saw the hand of a man on my right shoulder. As I expanded my awareness of this man's presence, I saw him standing on my right side with a happy smile on his face and an upbeat disposition. Interestingly, he was wearing a bathing suit with a white background, but it had red and green holiday designs all over it. To me, this appeared rather odd. He stood there with his arms outstretched toward Mary, absolutely full of love that was so overpowering it felt like my heart might burst. I sensed this man was her husband in spirit. I described what this man looked like and relayed everything I'd just seen and felt to Mary.

"Would you understand any of this?"

"Yes. You're right. That's my husband."

"He's presenting himself as middle-aged, perhaps in his late forties or early fifties. I'm running my hand along an imaginary timeline to see at what age he passed. I can't get past the fifties age bracket. This suggests to me he died in his fifties. Can you take this information?"

Mary's lips quivered. "That sounds exactly like Jim."

I continued on and began to focus on his personality. The more I focused on Jim's personality, character, and mannerisms, the more I felt this heightened sense of energy flow through me. I knew Jim was a very positive man who loved to help others and was just full of energy. I could tell he loved to talk, was quite expressive, and wore his emotions on his sleeves.

As I invited Jim's spirit to overshadow me, I began to fidget and couldn't sit still. I practically leaped out of my chair to stand and accommodate all the incoming energy I was feeling. I started to rub my hands together and soon was waving them sideways. At first it looked like I was throwing a Frisbee in an underhanded motion, but I soon brought my hands together and began to make motions like I was swinging a bat or perhaps chopping down a tree with an ax. Then I just started waving my hands in different, random ways.

"For some reason, I just feel I want to wave my arms wildly, but I didn't know why. Could any of these motions be significant in some way?"

"Yes, Jim always waved his hands wildly when he spoke."

One of the more endearing moments of the reading came when Mary's husband began giving me images of a fancy ballroom, fully decorated for the holidays and filled with joy and splendor. I saw many people on the dance floor dancing what appeared to be waltzes. Men were dressed in their suits and holiday finest, while the women wore long evening gowns, most of which were black or of various dark colors.

I stood next to Mary and her husband, who were dancing closely with each other and gazing into each other's eyes with smiles on their face. There was an overpowering sense of love between them and in the entire ballroom. Mary wore a long evening gown that looked black with a subtle hint of dark red in it. It felt soft, almost like velvet, and was quite a formal ball gown.

"Would you recognize this scene or understand its significance?"

"Yes, I remember that night well. I understand what it means."

I then saw Mary's husband wearing a bow tie, but it quickly changed to a long tie that had a white background with red and green holiday designs on it, similar to the bathing suit I saw at the beginning of the reading. To me, this white tie seemed completely out of place, but it felt important somehow. I described what I saw.

"This is a rather unusual tie. Would you understand it?"

Mary nodded vigorously. "Oh, yes. It's very significant. That was his favorite holiday tie, something he received from the choir he was in. He'd wear that to holiday parties."

I thought this was a another great example of spirit showing me a unique item that was significant to the sitter that only they would know.

As I took in the scene of the ballroom, I heard in my mind a snippet of the song "I Could Have Danced All Night" from the musical *The King And I.* I asked Mary if she understood this.

"Oh, my God. Yes. Jim was a big dancer. We loved to dance all the time, and we always went to holiday parties and danced." Mary had tears on her face at this point, and the love between these two people was palpable.

Then the scene of the ballroom just vanished. I started to see a bird take shape. It was red, midsized, and had a yellow beak and serious eyes. I thought this bird looked similar to a cardinal. The bird looked like it was in something clear, like a glass cage or a see-through pool. I didn't understand what it meant, so I kept looking at it to get more information. Inside this domed glass container I began to see gold flakes falling from the top that twirled around and sparkled as the light hit their different sides.

I simply described the image and asked Mary if this had any significance to her. Her eyes widened; she nodded and said cardinals were her husband's favorite bird, and she'd been receiving cardinals as gifts from all her friends. She pointed to one behind me that she said she liked for some reason. I turned around and saw this one perfectly matched what I was seeing. It was a cardinal in a large snow globe with sparkling golden flakes that would fall from the top spinning around after a person shook it up. Her husband really knew how to make an impression.

When I asked her husband for a message, I heard, "I'm still with you and always around you." I also heard him say, "I love you." I suddenly saw an image of Mary lying on her bed fast asleep, as her husband ethereally lay down next to her and lovingly wrapped his arms around her. I described this image to Mary.

"Would you understand this image your husband is giving me?"

"Yes, I often feel him lying next to me at night. Sometimes I feel a feather-light sensation, similar to a very light but warm blanket softly wrapped around me."

At the end of the reading, I felt and saw her husband begin to step back. I saw him softly waving his hand from side to side as he waved goodbye. I saw him blow a kiss to Mary, and then he vanished. I described this for her. All she could do was nod her head as she wiped the tears from her eyes.

"He always used those two gestures as his little sign to me. That's how he'd show his love to me and wave goodbye. Oh, God it's got meaning for me all right. I completely understand it."

After I closed the reading, we just sat there in contemplation of the beautiful session that had transpired and the love that had been shared. Mary's husband did a terrific job of communicating his love for her in such detailed and expressive ways. I felt touched just being the conduit of love between two such caring souls. I wish we all could be like that.

***

I hope these readings help you see not only the transformative love that spirit brings to our lives, but also how close spirit can be when it draws near. When a loved one passes from the physical to the nonphysical, they're not leaving us—they're just changing their energetic form. I always use the example of the butterfly: the caterpillar doesn't crawl into its cocoon and die—it emerges transformed as an even more beautiful butterfly. From crawling on the ground to flying away into space, we too transform. Remember, we're not human beings having a spiritual experience, we're spiritual beings having a human experience.

Afterword

I hope after reading this book, you have gained a new perspective on not only this life but the next. Spirit is always around us and remains very much alive, so we never have to mourn the passing of our loved ones, nor worry about our own physical death. While we may miss our loved ones here in the physical, which is natural, we should be overjoyed for them. They are now free from pain and feel joy and pure love, for they know the meaning of unconditional love and acceptance just for existing. They are happy, and they want you to be happy as well.

We should also consider how our actions affect our lives here on earth, the lives of others we impact, as well as our future life in spirit. Recall that we are all interconnected, as our lives are like threads of a giant tapestry which touch the lives of everyone around us. All our thoughts and deeds are felt by everyone else and ultimately come back and are felt by us. When we think of Jesus's command that we should love our neighbor as ourselves, he truly understood how the universe worked, given our interconnected energies.

The spirit world is constructed of love, for it's the very fabric of the afterlife. Spirit continually tries to deliver to us the message that we are loved more than we can ever know in this physical existence. Spirit also tries to remind us that we are never separated from each other or God because of that bond of love. This separation is just a trick of our ego mind. Separation is just an illusion, both because of infinite love and our universal interconnectedness. We are each a central part of the multiverse, and we each have the God Spark within us. Therefore, we become one with God.

Many people also believe in the separation between our thoughts, our mind and our body and that we cannot control what happens in our body. However, our thoughts, feelings and emotions are the most powerful energies in existence. Those energetic thoughts create vibrations that directly affect our mind and body, and they often are responsible for end products like disease. A loving and positive feeling about ourselves and others sends high frequency vibrations throughout our system and can result in wonderful results like a healthy mind and body. Conversely, negative and unloving emotions about ourselves often creates unhealthy results, such as depression and cancer. Many spontaneous remissions have been attributed to a flood of positive and loving thoughts. This makes perfect sense when one considers everything about the different human subtle bodies as previously discussed. Pay close attention to your thoughts, and remain positive and loving.

Spirit people are still alive, but have discarded their physical bodies and remain with their etheric bodies. As they have no ego, they are left with nothing but the love they had in the physical. The frequency of vibration from this love determines where we naturally fit in the spirit world. Imagine trying to enter a bright room that is so blindingly bright that it becomes too painful to enter, since our eyes aren't used to the light. Similarly, we don't want to enter onto a level with a vibration that's too high for us, as we're very uncomfortable with the frequency and brightness of the light. Consequently, we always arrive where we are supposed to be in the spirit world, due to natural law. So again, think positive and loving thoughts.

As you begin your own journey, you will encounter wonderful experiences that help expand your understanding and your heart. If you ask for their help, your spirit guides will aid you in your spiritual growth. Perhaps, like they did to me, they may put breadcrumbs on your path for you to follow and help your journey through the forest of knowledge and understanding.

Open your heart to spirit and send out a beacon of love. It will respond like a moth to the light, for spirit is attracted by love. You too can begin to communicate with spirit in an effort to help heal and comfort those in need. The more love you have in your heart, the stronger you will attract spirit and the more you can help others. We need to raise the vibration of this planet and help those who are still sleepwalking. Spirit is there to help us from their side, but we need to do our part on earth. Clearly the more we practice being loving to others in the physical, the more we grow our spirit here. In turn, we will more appreciate how important love is in the spirit world. That was a message that has come through loud and clear for me and one that I've now taken to heart. I hope you do too.

Love and Light,

—Chris Lippincott

FREE GUIDED MEDITATION

As a way of saying thank you for your purchase, I wanted to give you one of my guided meditations for FREE.
Click on the link below.

FREE GUIDED MEDITATION

What Did You Think of *Spirits Beside Us*?

First of all, thank you for purchasing my book ***Spirits Beside Us***. I know you could have picked any number of books to read, but you picked this book, and for that I am extremely grateful.

I hope that my book added value and quality to your everyday life. If so, I would truly appreciate it if you could share this book with your friends and family by posting to **Facebook** and **Twitter**.

If you enjoyed this book and found some benefit in reading this, I'd like to hear from you and hope that you could take some time to post a review on Amazon. Your feedback and support will help me to greatly improve my writing craft for future projects and make this book even better.

Please know that your review is very important. If you'd like to **leave a review**, all you have to do is click **below**. Go to the bottom of that page for reviews. I wish you all the best in your future success!

REVIEW

Reading List

Below is a reading list I compiled that is very helpful when trying to understand the afterlife. This includes academic studies, near-death experiences, automatic writings that give magnificent and detailed descriptions of the spirit world, reincarnation, mediumship, stories and experiences of mediums, and so much more. This list begins from an academic and scientific approach, moves on to automatic writings from spirit, and works its way through mediums and other experts. I've also tried to arrange the list and each section in a way that hopefully facilitates ease of understanding. Please understand this list barely scratches the surface of all the excellent research and publications available on afterlife studies. I strongly urge you to explore all the available material on this topic. Good reading.

ACADEMIC STUDIES, NEAR-DEATH EXPERIENCES, AND REINCARNATION

Life After Life by Raymond Moody, M.D.

Hello from Heaven: A New Field of Research-After-Death Communication Confirms that Life and Love Are Eternal by Bill Guggenheim and Judy Guggenheim

Irreducible Mind by Raymond Moody, M.D. & Dr. Bruce Greyson, M.D.

On Life After Death by Elizabeth Kubler-Ross, M.D.

Science and the Near-Death Experience by Chris Carter

Evidence of the Afterlife by Jeffrey Long, M.D.

Consciousness Beyond Life by Pim von Lommel, M.D.

The Art of Dying by Peter Fenwick and Elizabeth Fenwick

Proof of Heaven by Eben Alexander, M.D.

The Map of Heaven by Eben Alexander, M.D.

Journey of Souls: Case Studies of Life Between Lives by Michael Newton, Ph.D.

Many Lives, Many Masters: The True Story of a Prominent Psychiatrist by Brian Weiss, M.D.

The Quantum Enigma: Physics Encounters Consciousness by Bruce Rosenblum, Ph.D. & Fred Kutter, Ph.D.

A Lawyer Presents the Evidence for the Afterlife by Victor Zammit, M.A., Ph.D., LL.B.

To Heaven and Back by Mary C. Neal, M.D.

Dying To Be Me by Anita Moorjani

Embraced by the Light by Betty J. Eadie

AFTERLIFE DESCRIPTIONS FROM SPIRIT VIA AUTOMATIC WRITING

Letters From The Afterlife: A Guide to the Other Side by Elsa Barker

Parting Notes; A Connection With the Afterlife by April Crawford

Here and Hereafter by Anthony Borgia

Life in the World Unseen by Anthony Borgia

The Life Beyond the Veil Volume I—The Lowlands of Heaven by Rev. George Vale-Owen

The Life Beyond the Veil Volume II—The Highlands of Heaven by Rev. George Vale-Owen

The Life Beyond the Veil Volume III—The Ministry of Heaven by Rev. George Vale-Owen

The Life Beyond the Veil Volume IV—Battalions of Heaven by Rev. George Vale-Owen

The Life Beyond the Veil Volume V—Outlands of Heaven by Rev. George Vale-Owen

Spirit World and Spirit Life by Charlotte Dresser

Life Here and Hereafter by Charlotte Dresser

Through the Mists by Robert James Lees

The Life Elysian by Robert James Lees

The Padgett Messages—The True Gospel Revealed Anew by Jesus by James E. Padgett

Spirit Teachings by William Stanton Moses

Gone West: Three Narratives of After Death Experiences by J.S.M Ward

A Sublatern in Spirit Land by J. S. M. Ward

The Blue Island by Pardoe Woodman and Estelle Stead

Testimony of Light: An Extraordinary Message of Life After Death by Helen Greaves

The Book of James by Susy Smith

Ghost Writers in the Sky by Susy Smith

The Seth Material by Jane Roberts

MEDIUMISTIC DESCRIPTIONS OF SPIRIT AND THE AFTERLIFE

Adventures of the Soul: Journeys Through the Physical and Spiritual Dimension by James Van Praagh

The Power of Love by James Van Praagh

The Light Between Us: Stories From Heaven. Lessons for the Living by Laura Lynn Jackson

The Happy Medium by Kim Russo

You Can't Make This Stuff Up: Life Changing Lessons From Heaven by Theresa Caputo

Survival of the Soul by Lisa Williams

Embracing Eternity by Tony Stockwell

Where Two Worlds Meet by Janet Nohavec

Bridging Two Realms by John Holland

The Afterlife Revealed: What Happens After We Die by Michael Tymn

The Afterlife Unveiled: What the Dead are Telling Us About Their World by Stafford Betty

My Two Worlds by Gladys Leonard

The Fun of Dying by Roberta Grimes

Love and a Map to the Unaltered Soul by Tina Louise Spalding

Life Beyond Death: What Should We Expect by David Fontana

Soul Smart by Suzanne Wilson

How to Meet and Work with Spirit Guides by Ted Andrews

Wisdom from Your Spirit Guides: A Handbook to Contact Your Soul's Greatest Teachers by James Van Praagh

Keys to the Spirit World: An Easy to Use Handbook for Contacting Your Spirit Guides by Jennifer O'Neill

Notes

INTRODUCTION

1 Martin Twycross, CSNU "Developing Mediumship" http://www.develo pingmediumship.co.uk/how-to-develop/

DEATH IS NOT GOODBYE

2 William James, *Writings* 1902–1910 *The Varieties of Religious Experience/ Pragmatism/A Pluralistic Universe/The Meaning of Truth/Some Problems of Philosophy/Essays.*(New York: Library of America), 1264.

THE HUMAN SUBTLE ENERGY SYSTEM

3 Jackie Allen, "Chakra Healing Basics." *Psychic Elements,* February 6, 2015, https://psychicelements.com/blog/chakra-healing/

THE SPIRIT REALMS

4 Victor Zammit and Wendy Zammit,*A Lawyer Presents the Evidence for the Afterlife.*(United Kingdom: White Crow Books, 2013).

5 Anthony Borgia, *Here and Hereafter.*

6 John Milton, *Paradise Lost.*(Indianapolis: Hackett Publishing Company, Inc., 2005): bk I, lines 221–270

7 Siddartha Guatama, *DhammapadaSutra.*(Compiled by Michael P. Garofalo, 2009): Chapter 1, verse 1

8 James E. Padgett, *The Padgett Messages vols 1–5,* edited by Klaus Fuchs 2017

9 *ibid.* Padgett, *The Padgett Messages*

10 *ibid.*

11 *ibid.*

12 *ibid.*

13 Peter Dizikes, "When the Butterfly Effect Took Flight." *MIT Technology Review,* February 22, 2011, https://www.technologyreview.com/s/4228

09/when-the-butterfly-effect-took-flight/.

THE DIFFERENCES BETWEEN SPIRIT GUIDES AND ANGELS

14 https://www.merriam-webster.com/dictionary/, s.v. "arch"

ANYONE CAN COMMUNICATE WITH SPIRIT

15 Patilla, Mavis. https://www.mavispittilla.com/teaching/

COMMUNICATION CONCEPTS

16 Martin Twycross, CSNU "Developing Mediumship" http://www.develo pingmediumship.co.uk/how-to-develop/

About the Author

Chris Lippincott is a practicing psychic medium whose evidential readings and unique information from spirit helps transform people's lives. Chris has trained with some of the world's greatest teaching mediums. He has studied with tutors from England's Arthur Findlay College and the Spiritualists' National Union International, including Tony Stockwell, Martin Twycross, Rev. Janet Nohavec, James Van Praagh, and Lee VanZyl.

While aware of spirit as a child, it wasn't until after a profound spiritual awakening later in life that Chris began to connect with spirit and develop his abilities to communicate. Chris discovered that his passion is providing comfort, healing and the knowledge that our loved ones in spirit are alive and well and still care about us.

Chris is a husband and father who lives in a New Jersey suburb outside of New York City.

You can connect with me on:

https://montclairmedium.com

https://twitter.com/MontClairMedium

https://www.facebook.com/montclairmedium/?tn-str=k*F

Subscribe to my newsletter:

https://montclairmedium.com/contact

Made in United States
North Haven, CT
24 July 2022

21760784R00135